Wade in the Water

TAHARKAH X

ISBN: 1-4392-4041-8
EAN13: 9781439240410

Visit www.booksurge.com to order additional copies.

For my darling Wife L, Auntie M, & Old Man W.

"It is only in his music, which Americans are able to admire because a protective sentimentality limits their understanding of it, that the Negro in America has been able to tell his story."

—James Baldwin

We are unable to conclusively confirm the existence of the mythical figure known as William Lynch. He is alleged to have been both a slave owner and an expert in psychology. According to folklore, Lynch devised a system to manipulate Afrikan[1] people's minds for the purpose of making us better slaves. His program of physical, sexual, and psychological torture is believed to be outlined in documents known as the Willie Lynch Letter and The Willie Lynch Papers. Excerpts from the Letter first became popularized during a poignant sermon given by the Minister Louis Farrakhan during the Million Man March in 1995. We are also able to find references to Willie Lynch in papers supposedly published by the "Black Arcade Liberation Library" in 1970. Our efforts to verify the existence of such a library or even the organization itself have been fruitless. The language of the letter itself is suspect. It bears a stronger resemblance to modern American English than that of the 1700's. The Willie Lynch papers nevertheless remain an important sociological text for Afrikan people everywhere. The details in the Papers bear a chilling resemblance to the program which has been enacted against Afrikan people all over the world. "Willie Lynch" is therefore an effective and convenient euphemism for the institutionalized denial of Black humanity and all of its horrific effects. The scars that this regimen has

---

1   We invoke our right to name ourselves and have opted for the Traditionalist spelling of both "Africa" and "African" throughout the course of our presentation.

I

left upon Afrikan society are absolutely verifiable. It is also painfully evident that scores of Black people perpetuate this system to serve their own selfish interests. We have included one of the many versions of the letter for the benefit of those unfamiliar with its contents:

GENTLEMEN:

I greet you here on the bank of the James River in the year of our Lord, one thousand seven hundred and twelve. First I shall thank you, the Gentlemen of the Colony of Virginia, for bringing me here. I am here to help you solve some of your problems with slaves. Your invitation reached me on my modest plantation in the West Indies where I have experimented with some of the newest and still the oldest methods for control of slaves. Ancient Rome would envy us if my program is implemented. As our boat sailed south on the James River, named for our illustrious King James, whose bible we cherish, I saw enough to know that your program is not unique. While Rome used cords of wood as crosses for standing human bodies along the old highways in great numbers, you are here using the tree and the rope on occasion.

I caught the whiff of a dead slave hanging from a tree a couple of miles back. You are not only losing valuable stock by hangings, you are having uprisings, slaves are running away, your crops are sometimes left in the fields too long for maximum profit, you suffer occasional fires, your animals are killed, gentlemen...you know what your problems are; I do not need to elaborate. I am not here to enumerate your problems, I am here to introduce you to a method of solving them.

In my bag here, I have a fool-proof method for controlling your black slaves. I guarantee everyone of you that if installed correctly it will control the slaves for at least 300 years. My method is simple, any member of your family or any overseer can use it.

II

I have outlined a number of differences among the slaves, and I take these differences and make them bigger. I use fear, distrust, and envy for control purposes. These methods have worked on my modest plantation in the West Indies, and it will work throughout the South. Take this simple little test of differences and think about them. On the top of my list is "Age", but it is there because it only starts with an "A"; the second is "Color" or shade; there is intelligence, size, sex, size of plantations, attitude of owners, whether the slaves live in the valley, on a hill, East, West, North, South, have fine or coarse hair, or is tall or short. Now that you have a list of differences, I shall give you an outline of action--but before that, I shall assure you that distrust is stronger than trust, and envy is stronger than adulation, respect, or admiration.

The Black Slave, after receiving this indoctrination, shall carry on and will become self refueling and self generating for hundreds of years, maybe thousands.

Don't forget, you must pitch the old Black vs. the young Black male, and the young Black male against the old Black male. You must use the dark skinned slaves vs. the light skinned slaves, and the light skinned slaves vs. the dark skinned slaves. You must use the female vs. the male, and the male vs. the female. You must also have your servants and overseers distrust all Blacks, but it is necessary that your slaves trust and depend on us. They must love, respect, and trust only us.

Gentlemen, these kits are your keys to control, use them. Have your wives and children use them. Never miss opportunity. My plan is guaranteed, and the good thing about this plan is that if used intensely for one year, the slaves themselves will remain perpetually distrustful.

—From the Willie Lynch Letter of 1712

Would "Willie Lynch" be content with the condition of our people today? He certainly would find that there were glitches in his plan. These "glitches" are the formidable will, intelligence, talent and imagination of Afrikan people all over the world. "Willie Lynch" did not expect that we would become educated. Under the "Lynch" program, Black people were supposed to be reduced to the level of savages. Fighting one another and showing off were supposed to be our ultimate goals in life, not going to school. Our quest for access to education is well-documented. They simply could not stop us from learning. Even the racist reporters of Reconstruction Era South Carolina had to admit that 'black children love the school as white children love a holiday'. Education freed us from blind reliance on the word of our oppressors. Not only were we able to find the answers for ourselves, but we were able to manipulate and expand upon the available information for our benefit. "Willie" would definitely raise an eyebrow at a brother such as Dr. Charles Drew. That a Black scientist would discover that by refrigerating them separately, blood plasma and blood substance could be stored for longer periods of time (or "banked") was not part of the "Willie Lynch" plan. Michael P. Anderson's orbiting the Earth more than 100 times and Dr. Patricia Bath's pioneering laser optical surgery reveal further flaws in the conspiracy. But formal education was not the sole stake in the shriveled heart of our nemesis. He was not expecting that we would continue to love our history. And we do. From the repatriation of Afrikan American and Caribbean Blacks in Ghana (approximately 3000 as of 2006) to the definitive ancestral DNA tests of today, Afrikan people have never stopped wondering about our heritage. This is not because Black people wish to live in some mythical past, but because we are a people who value the wisdom of our elders and ancestors. Whatever jewels we are able to glean and reclaim along our journey in search of self are worth the trip. "Willie" could not have imagined that we would learn of or even care about the ancient pyramids near the Congo basin. He never could have dreamed that in 2009, we would still marvel at the scientifically astute creation theories of the Dogon people (Mali) and the spectacular ivory work of the Bamileke (Cameroon). Our love for one another was another hole in the conspiracy. "Lynch" would have had a heart attack during the 1968 Olympics when Tommie Smith and John Carlos called attention on the plight of our people by giving the world the Black Power Salute. The Free Breakfast Program sponsored and operated by the Oakland branch of the Black Panther Party (1969) was not the actions of a people who hated and distrusted one another. It was the work of a free and responsible people. The gathering of hundreds of thousands of law-abiding, concerned Afrikan men at the Million Man March in 1995 was no different. These are just a few examples. But if "Willie" did not have an aneurism by 1995, the newest Afrikan nation of Somaliland would definitely kill him. Journalists from CNN scratched their heads in amazement as they reported in 2006 on this peaceful, strong breakaway country. Somaliland broke away from war-torn Somalia in 1991 and has managed to form a stable and prosperous country without a single dollar of international aid. News clips of Black people pushing wheelbarrows full of cold cash down the street in broad daylight, unmolested by their brothers and sisters are rare in the mainstream. But there they were.

The bravery of Nat Turner, Harriet Tubman, or the Los Angeles branch of the Black Panther Party who held off an entire police force for days were also devastating blows to the house of cards that is the Willie Lynch plan. We were supposed to be cowards.

A quick glance at our history proves that we are not. Old School rap music is another example of the virtue and tenacity of Afrikan men and women. Instead of exhibiting hatred and a desire to exterminate our people, Grandmaster Flash warned us all to stay clear of the narcotics trap (*White Lines*). Run DMC's *Proud to Be Black* was of a similar spirit. Public Enemy was not a band of sniveling, frightened Negroes fainting away at the sight of their own shadows. Their intelligent militarism was not in line with the mentality espoused in the Lynch papers.

One thing that "Willie Lynch" failed to consider was the soundtrack of Black music that accompanied every victory and setback that we experienced. Even if he had taken note of our music, he never could have perceived it as a threat. His aim was to make Afrikan people flee from our natural selves. We were supposed to fear and abhor our Blackness. Yet we clung with iron fists to the musical legacy of our original home. Our music ensures that we need never be separated from Afrika. We are able to summon and visit Her at any time simply by tapping into our Soul. Nor would "Lynch" have been able to predict the world's response to Black music. The entire globe is captivated by our unique and charismatic culture. It is now impossible to speak of musical "culture" these days without mentioning Black men and women. From the German's love of parroting Afrikan American break dancers to pop artists who "rap" in Chinese, Black people are easily the most emulated people in the world today. People in rural parts of the Middle East and Asia may not have heard of Beethoven, but they know how to moonwalk. Americans prefer Black music (Rock 'n Roll, Blues, Hip Hop) to European music. In 2008, Andrew Vactor of Urbana, Ohio received a ticket for violation of the city's noise ordinance. He was blasting rap music in his car. The judge gave him the option of listening to classical music or paying a $150 fine. He chose to pay the fine!

Returning to our question, would "Willie Lynch" feel that his plan has been defeated? Absolutely not. The "Lynch" doctrine calls for physical and psychological containment of the Afrikan race. But he does not specify the size of the "plantation", nor does he explicitly state the manner in which the methods of psychological terrorism would be employed. Thus, "plantation" could mean a city, country, or even an entire continent. The "Lynch" program allows for great flexibility of method and practice because the descriptions given by the alleged author are so vague. At its foundation, the "Lynch" plan simply calls for the following: that Afrikan people perpetuate hatred of self and kind in order to reduce us to a state of perpetual mental servitude so that we are constantly available for economic exploitation. It is entirely possible to be educated and wealthy and yet in the grips of a system of psychological and physical containment that is self-perpetuating. Despite its nationalist, unifying, and supportive roots, rap music has become the voice of such a system. It has become the perfect vehicle for transmitting messages of self-loathing and hatred towards the Black race in general. And there is a bonus. In addition to eroding the foundation of Black unity and self-love, rap lyrics also invite the rest of the planet to disrespect, exploit, and abuse us all. Through it, mental slavery has now become fashionable.

Our bondage today differs in many ways from what our ancestors experienced. Our ancestors greeted slavery with terror and rage. They prayed and sobbed as they caught their last glances of the glistening pale sands of West Afrikan beaches. But this time there is no wailing from the bowels of the slave ships, no desperate pleas for intercession from Allah, Shango, Oshun, or Tongnaab. Modern slavery is accepted with the belief that this "deathstyle[2]" is sanctioned by our religions. Why else would rappers and thugs put God's Name in the middle of their genocidal ramblings? Today there is no hiding, no running from the fate that befell our brothers, mothers, and neighbors. Our ancestors learned to avoid Europeans and other Afrikan societies known to deal in human cargo. Today's slaves deliberately seek out those who wish to annihilate us. There will be no soul-wrenching cries as children, sisters, and brothers are sold down the river this time. The new slaves cheer as dysfunctional Black families tear each other apart on the talk shows. This time there will be no struggle against the irons. Indeed, chains have become symbols of masculinity and/or womanhood. Being manacled and shuffled off to prison or the county jail is a symbol of strength to today's slaves. It shows that he or she a real motherfucker, a down ass bitch, a *real nigga*. And anyone who dares to raise their voice against this tirade of raunchiness, death, and wasted potential is labeled a "hater".

Happily, the notion that this modern minstrel show rules the heart of Black culture is false. It is important to make the distinction between reality and the mere appearance of things. Though some may find it difficult to believe, there are scores of Afrikan people that understand that we will never rise above the level of our thoughts. These intelligent Black people applaud only those parts of popular culture that celebrate life and honor our heritage. We come from all walks of life. We are teachers, parents, church members, athletes, entertainers,

---

2   Opposite of a "lifestyle" because it opposes the growth and change necessary to sustain life.

Christians, Hebrews, Traditionalists[3], college students, and blue collar workers. We are South Afrikans, Ghanaians, Puerto Ricans, Nigerians, Afrikan Americans, Jamaicans, Brazilians, Britons and Norwegians. In these tempestuous times, we take to the wisdom of our heritage as a port in the storm. Our people possess extensive knowledge of the human soul's journey to its rightful place at the side of its Divine Beloved. We navigate difficult times with faith, humor, and when necessary, all forms of resistance. We are human beings and we love that which magnifies human life. What we witness from the hip hop world is a role reversal. The popular rapper rejects the divine crown of humanity. He or she promotes a life of eating, sleeping, hoarding, rutting and violence without regard for the pain of millions of victims. These victims include abused Black women, innocent bystanders that were murdered as a result of gang activity, abandoned Black and interracial children and people that have been robbed or had their homes invaded.

This does not mean that we are incapable of understanding and empathizing with the condition of modern slaves. Those us of who are lost in the hip hop mentality are that way for a reason. To some degree, we have all suffered the same sort of abuse, disappointments, financial distress, anger and pain that they presently endure. Through these unwanted and seemingly undeserved trials, we have learned that there is nowhere to go but here. We cannot escape ourselves. There is no running away from the Universal Laws. Like attracts like. If we want this life to be

3   The term "Afrocentric" is closely associated with the study of Ancient Egypt/Kemet. We offer the term "Traditionalist" to denote the cultural traditions of Afrikans displaced by the TransAtlantic Slave trade and those West & Central Afrikan nations from which they descend.

beautiful, we must endeavor to make it so. It is for this reason that our Afrikan ancestors invented music. This is why they danced in the desert and in clearings in the Equatorial forests. Real Black music rouses the spirit. It serves as spiritual armor against the chill of mortality and the pain associated with human societies. Our music points out what is fine in life. The singer (or rapper) uses his voice as a key, releasing the bolts on the beautiful places in our souls. In these "beautiful places", we find the relief of reunion, the saving wisdom that arrives when pain recedes, the freedom and ecstasy of sexuality, the seeds of invention and the all-consuming tides of love and life. After communing with Afrikan Soul, one walks away feeling that 'everything is gonna be alright'. Black music soothes us. It does not matter whether it is Toni Braxton moaning over a lost love, Count Basie urging us to "Jump for Me" on the dance floor, or Miriam Makeba's sensual flirtation in *Pata Pata*. Afrikan music teaches us that whether we understand it or not, everything that happens is sent by the Divine Beloved for our own good. As soon as we learn our lesson from an experience, we are freed from the pain of it. It's going to be alright. Wade in the water, children. Turn your backs on the modern day plantation and all of its scandal. Wash off the stain of ignorance, violence, and filth promoted by those in the hip hop and R&B world who care nothing at all for our health, happiness, or progress. Wade in the water, brothers. Pull up your trousers. You are not clowns, niggas, dawgs or cockroaches. You are men. Wade in the water, sisters. There will be places where the water gets deep (and not just knee deep). We must put the children on our shoulders and carry them across. Teach them not to look back at the shiny automobiles, gold teeth, and half naked women prostituting themselves for worthless things that glitter. Warn them that their beautiful hearts will turn to stone. The "water" is our culture. It is powerful, generous, life-sustaining water. The water is our heritage and our strength. It can remove the pain. It can dissolve the filth. As our wise ancestors said, *God's gonna trouble the water.*

WADE IN THE WATER

CHAPTER ONE

Identity: Of Masks and Men

"The black slave, after receiving this indoctrination, shall carry on and will become self-refueling and self-generating for hundreds of years, maybe thousands."

—From the Willie Lynch Letter

"The fact is, I don't have any experience of being a slave. However, 246 years of protracted slavery guaranteed the prosperity and privilege of the south's white progeny while correspondingly relegating its black progeny to a legacy of debt and suffering. It doesn't really matter today if either of us, black or white, directly experienced or participated in slavery. What does matter is that African Americans have experienced a *legacy* of trauma...The legacy of trauma is reflected in many of our behaviors and our beliefs; behaviors and beliefs that were at one time necessary to adopt in order to survive, yet today serve to undermine our ability to be successful."

—Dr. Joy DeGruy Leary, Ph.D.

Cultural Identity of Afrikans in the United States

What drove our people in the 1980's to push for the legalization of the term "African American" when it is obvious that we have been away from Africa for hundreds of years? What evidence legitimizes our claim of Afrikan heritage and culture? It is undeniable that Afrikan American life is infused with

1

Euro-American notions and values. Nonetheless, we maintain that our culture is a continuation and a variation of West and Central Afrikan cultural traditions. Acknowledging our true heritage does not mean that we reject America. Nor is it expressive of hatred towards other Americans. Black people have invested millions of lives and countless hours of our own labor to build this country and we intend to enjoy America and all of its perks. We know very well that an Afrikan man named Crispus Attucks was the first person to die in the Revolutionary War against Britain. He died in 1770 while leading a protest march in Boston. We are the ones who cleared the forests (even 4'10" tall Harriet Tubman worked as a lumberjack while enslaved) and tilled the land in this country. This is obviously something that Caucasians were incapable of doing. Why else would they bother capturing and torturing nearly 100 million human souls for 300 years? We are proud of our strong, intelligent ancestors because their labor paved the way for our many achievements in this country. This should not be interpreted as gratitude for slavery. Nor do we feel that "the end justifies the means". We are proud of the ways in which they coped with their new situations- not the conditions that caused them to be here in the first place. Afrikan American people provided America with thousands of miles of railroad tracks as the country expanded westwards. We fought under the American flag by the thousands in Vietnam even though in 1969, Caucasian soldiers in Danang and Cam Ranh Bay burned crosses to celebrate the assassination of Dr. Martin Luther King, Jr. Afrikans such as Jackie Robinson and Muhammad Ali endured tremendous racial hatred and even physical assaults. Yet they brought America great acclaim with their grit and extraordinary talent. Our people formed the backbone of America's automotive and manufacturing industries from the 1950's until the industrial crash in the 1980's. Scores of hardworking, tax-paying, patriotic Afrikan Americans toiled in Chrysler, General Motors, and General Electric factories throughout the Midwestern United States. Our continuous assertion of an Afrikan identity is neither a blind refusal to assimilate, nor is it based in ideas of racial purity. Those types of ideas are not of Afrikan origin. Afrikan Americans were not the ones who invented the ridiculous racial categories of the American South. Black people did not make up the titles "quadroon" (meaning one-fourth Black) and "octoroon" (one-eighth Black). We did not institute the "paper bag" rule, whereby a person was judged according to whether or not he was lighter in color than a brown paper bag. If the young reader is unfamiliar with these terms, it is because many of these racial designations are no longer in use. We all laughed in October of 2008 when Andy Lacasse of Florida proudly displayed a home-made sign in his front yard that described Barack Obama as a "half-breed muslin [sic]".

From the highly adaptive and endlessly expressive genre of Jazz to Rock 'n Roll and its spontaneously provocative and soothing rhythm to Blues, Soul, R&B and hip hop, we continue to stir cultural gems into the American soup. Even country music is laced with Afrikan elements. The drumming and Rock underpinnings of today's country music is what distinguishes it from its European roots. But for our people, country music would still sound much "Oh, Susanna" and other banjo solos brought here by German settlers. It is true that our people invented these musical genres using European instruments. Necessity is the mother of invention. Our people used what was available to them at the time. Saying that we were introduced to the saxophone in America is correct. It is incorrect, however, to claim that America "gave" us the saxophone or anything else for that matter. We did not come here as cultural exchange students. We were given no gifts upon our arrival. Our people expanded the ways in which these instruments were used, giving them a distinctly West Afrikan flavor. Afrikans brought the Western world the gift of our musical theory. Music was important to our enslaved forebears because it is illustrative of the Afrikan social structure. Through it, they were able to create an Afrikan village away from home.

For our people, sound is not just for the ears. Certain sounds have *their own smells* as well! We remain Afrikans because we carry Afrika's cultural and genetic stamp. A sliver of the golden Afrikan sun shines through every one of our achievements, inventions, and innovations. This "sliver" has made all the difference for us. The flexibility of the Afrikan psyche is what allows us to be both Afrikan and American without feeling a sense of contradiction. Our people never wanted to come to America, but once here, we gave this country our all. Did our beloved ancestors Ben, Daniel, and Harry not toil for weeks on end to build the White House without receiving a thin dime? We are not the ones who said that Afrikan people were not also Americans. It was the Constitution of the United States that said we were only three-fifths of a human being. It was Caucasian Americans who said that we should never be free, vote, go to school, or use certain hospitals, restrooms, and drinking fountains. We have bombed no churches in this country. We have burned no crosses nor have we lynched in this country. We rarely see them, but we are committed to the ideals of freedom and prosperity that inform America's notions of itself. Yet we remain Afrikan people in the same way that people from China continue to be Chinese even if they have been in America for five generations.

One easily recognizable remnant our Afrikan heritage is the now widely popular dialect of Ebonics. In his 1979 op-ed piece entitled *Black English,* James Baldwin wrote that language "reveals the private identity, and connects one with, or divorces one from, the larger, public, or communal identity"[4]. Black people in the Diasporas descend from speakers of Ewe, Yoruba, Igbo, Mossi, Mende, Wolof, Temne, etc. Each group had its own language. But they were fated to leave Afrika together, enduring the physical and psychological horrors of the Middle Passage and toiling in the same American forests and plantations side by side. Our people had to devise some system of communication that would allow them to understand each other. This often took place on slave vessels. Afrikans would learn the language of the most numerous ethnic group on board. The most famous example of this is the Amistad revolt of 1839, when Mende-speaking Afrikans taught members of the Komo, Gbandi, and Temne clans to speak their language during the Middle Passage. In the United States and the Caribbean, our people created Ebonics to retain a sliver of their Afrikan sensibilities. They spoke English with a West Afrikan accent and so do we. We held on to the rhythm and cadence, if not the vocabulary, of our original languages. Speaking Ebonics reveals us as descendants of those who survived American apartheid. It connects us to the creators of a vast portion of the world's sense of culture. Most Afrikan Americans are adept at 'code-switching', wherein we speak Ebonics in informal social settings and standard American English for business and commerce. The very words that are used all over the world to describe our

---

4   New York Times, July 1979.

inventions are Ebonics terms. "Break dancing" is a Jamaican term that was coined in the earliest days of rap. "Jazz" is a sexual reference used by Afrikan people in New Orleans. Ebonics is not "broken English". We find it telling that this terminology is never applied to Caucasian people who speak English with a South African (Afrikaner) or Australian accent. Neither dialect is considered "proper" English. Yet when people of color have our own manner of speaking a European language, we are speaking "slang" or a "pidgin" or "talking ghetto". It is also amazing how our "broken" English magically becomes "fixed" when newscasters, advertisers, and even politicians want to borrow words and phrases from Ebonics. "Don't go there", "Getting our groove on", "talk to the hand" and a number of other Ebonics expressions are picked up by the media and carried into the mainstream. Those that non-Blacks find "cute" or hip become part of the American lexicon. Those that they are unable to appreciate or understand are labeled "ghetto".

Ebonics encompasses all forms of communication. It is made up of words, postures, gestures, expressions, and seemingly nonsensical sounds that carry specific meanings. Beat-boxing is definitely one of the most famous examples. Rappers such as Doug E. Fresh and Darren Robinson (also known as the Human Beat Box from the popular trio, the Fat Boys) use their lips, tongues, cheeks, and throats to create melodies. This recalls our captive forbears' knack for improvising instruments out of ordinary items such as bottles and hair combs. We do not need instruments. Wherever we go, we carry the drum inside our souls.

It is important to note that Ebonics contains words from West and Central Afrikan languages. We frequently use these words in ordinary conversation. Don't we refer to music, clothing, and certain situations as 'funky'? And isn't the word 'funky' a variation of the Congolese adjective '*lu-fuki*', which means "foul-smelling"? No one used that word until our Afrikan ancestors brought it to the West. The same is true of the words 'cooter' (for 'turtle) and "goober' (for 'peanut'). The word 'bogus' comes from the Congo ('*boko-boko*' means 'fake'). Afrikan American and Caribbean Blacks also continue to eat yams (from the Nigerian word '*nyama*') and okra (also Nigerian in origin), both of which were unknown in United States before being brought here by our ancestors. There are roughly one hundred other such borrowings and alterations in the Ebonics lexicon.

We dare not deny that we are Americans, Jamaicans, or British. To do so would mean disregarding the tremendous sacrifices of our ancestors that toiled incessantly and without compensation in the fields, forests, and on the railroads for most of this country's history. We are the inheritors of their legacy of strength. We have also inherited a powerful social structure. In order to appreciate just how low popular Black culture has fallen, we must start at the beginning. We must examine the basic elements of the culture that gave us the world's greatest music and made us a nation of survivors. The three basic principles of this social structure (and therefore the Afrikan identity) are communalism, ancestral reverence, and self-preservation.

Communalism

Communalism emphasizes sharing and group ownership. This is a dominant feature of West Afrikan culture. Native

American societies also operated along these lines. This is very different from European culture which is competitive and encourages individual hoarding and stockpiling. "Call and response", one of the distinguishing characteristics of our music, reminds us of the communalism in our original cultures. Aretha Franklin's song *Respect* comes easily to mind as an example. Whatever Ms. Franklin says in the song is "responded" to by the backup singer's world-famous "Woop!" Aretha Franklin is the lead singer on the song, but without the "Woop!" it simply ain't *lu-fuki*! In hip hop music, when the lead rapper to tell us to "Lean wit' it", we reply "Rock wit' it!" We sing and rap as a group. We participate. We respond. In places such as Nigeria and Mali, the groom's relatives refer to a new bride as "our wife". They do not mean that the woman is now married to everybody in the husband's family. The term merely reflects the bride's position as an integral part of her new family. In Afrika, the words "I" and "mine" are not used as often as "we" and "ours". Ghanaians refer to all older female relative as "mother". Older male relatives are called "uncle". These older relatives in turn refer to younger people as their sons and daughters. The emphasis is away from the biological mother and father, moving the "ownership" of the child into the realm of group activity. The communal nature of Afrikan American culture once offered an inclusiveness that eludes us in today's society. We did not need to be rich, popular, or filled with silicone. We just needed to be Black. Our Blackness was a passport to a world of wise advice, outstretched helping hands and humor that could bring laughter on some of the worst days. We supported one another.

The selfless acts of the noble Afrikan Americans of Montgomery, Alabama provide a flawless representation of the power of community. In the southern United States, Black people could only use public transportation if we sat in the back of the bus. If a Caucasian boarded and there were no empty seats, we were required to give up our seat and stand for the rest of the ride. In 1954, a 15 year-old sister named Claudette Colvin was arrested for sitting at the front of the bus. The following year, an 18 year old sister was jailed on similar offenses. These are just two of the many Afrikan Americans who were beaten by mobs or roughed up by the police for daring to behave like any other paying customer on the bus. Our beloved Rosa Parks was arrested for "disorderly conduct" in December of that same year. She took her case to court and was convicted. The very next day, the citizens of Montgomery staged a one-day test boycott to see how effective it would be. 9 out of 10 Afrikans stayed off the buses. One day without the revenue that thousands of paying Black customers bring forced the city officials to the negotiating table. They met with our leaders to discuss a compromise. This "deal" was in reality nothing but a repackaging of the existing laws. Our people saw right through it. The Mississippi Improvement Association began to organize car pools. The Boycott was on. Ordinary citizens became heroes. People woke up early and went out of their way to drive children to school. Church buses set out before dawn, crammed with brothers and sisters on their way to work. Black people drove until we ran out of gas. We drove until our tires were bald. When there was no one to give us a ride, we walked. Hundreds of Afrikan men, women, and children chose to walk and retain their dignity rather than ride and be treated like second-class citizens. They walked all year round; through the cold winters and hot, humid summers. We had decided as a community that we were not going to pay the city while it treated us like slaves. We did not resume riding the buses in Montgomery until we were granted equal treatment.

Our music is a reflection of the dominating issues of its time. When we were boycotting the buses in Alabama, there was a soundtrack of music to keep our spirits buoyed during those long walks to work. The brothers at the 1968 Olympics had the heart to salute us because our culture saluted them. It celebrated their Blackness and educated them on the struggle. James Brown told us to be proud of ourselves and our heritage. Berry Gordy started the Motown label in 1960. Motown pushed our culture to the forefront, raising the spirits of millions of Afrikan people worldwide. Old School rap music was no different. Run DMC make references to rapping for charity on their track *My Adidas*. Kurtis Blow was fiercely anti-drug. *White Lines* decries the choices that lead to addiction. They were not simply rapping about themselves and their possessions. Paying charity decreases desperation. Less desperation equals less crime. Drug use only benefits dope pushers and the government. The common people are the ones who end up paying for it, either through taxes or as victims of crime. These brothers had our best interests at heart. They used their visibility to look after our people. This is different from today's rap. With the exception of a handful of rappers, these so-called "artists" are nothing but slave catchers. They are anti-communal. Anyone who is mindless enough to get caught up in their filthy tales of greed and hatred of all things Afrikan becomes a cog in the system that was designed to destroy us. They become indoctrinated in an extremely selfish mindset that is most unlike the values that nurtured our Civil Rights leaders.

Ancestral Reverence

Wisdom does not develop in a vacuum. We are the culmination of the intellectual and spiritual experiences of the former generations. So dependent are we upon the knowledge of our ancestors that we implement their ideas without thinking. Our West and Central Afrikan ancestors never worried about their livestock being wiped out by disease. This is because their ancestors learned to space out their flocks. Splitting up their animals and placing them twenty or thirty miles apart decreased the chance of sicknesses spreading rapidly and decimating their sources of meat and (in some cases) milk. This gave our people a greater chance of survival than the generations that had kept their herds all in one place. They enjoyed a longer lifespan than those before them. They owed all this to the wisdom of their ancestors. Similarly, Afrikan people in America enjoy a great many advantages thanks to the wit and perseverance of our forbears. We never even think about giving up our seat on the bus to someone just because they are Caucasian. We don't have to get off of the sidewalk and stare at the gutter when they pass us on the streets. We are able to attend America's beautiful universities and lose ourselves amid stacks of rare books in the library. We owe all of this to our ancestors and the beautiful culture that inspired them. For this reason, ancestors and elders have always enjoyed high status in West Afrikan societies. Anthropologists call this "ancestral reverence". This feature of our original culture is a point of strength. Recognizing that we share ancestry (and therefore blood) allows us to see ourselves as one people. Ancient West Afrikan villages were founded by brothers and sisters that claimed lineage from the same female ancestor. A steady stream of new spouses, in-laws, employees, and family friends would swell their numbers until they had a population large enough to be self-sufficient.

The significance of ancestral reverence must not be overlooked! We must have heroes that 1) are Afrikan and 2) are people who actually cared about us. Today's R&B is anti-historical. Mainstream rap is anti-ancestral. Instead of telling our story, post-Pride[5] entertainers praise criminals such as John Gotti. They compare themselves to racist Caucasian gangs like the Mafia. There are tales from Mali that would make a quantum physicist drop his jaw. The slave narratives are overflowing with tales of bravery, selflessness, romance, and sweet revenge. The rapper could tell these tales. Yet today's slave rappers use their visibility to praise non-Afrikans who couldn't care less about us. As the Willie Lynch letter states *"... it is necessary that your slaves trust and depend on us. They must love, respect, and trust only us."* The slave catchers in rap and R&B use their charisma to lull our brains to sleep. Scores of our people foolishly drool over the diamond-studded watches around their wrists, never realizing that the shackles are tightening around their own necks and ankles. Rap ignores the sacrifices of our people. We were not welcome in the recording studios in this country until the artists of the past dazzled the world with their talent. They did not receive the incredible dividends that Black rappers and R&B singers enjoy today. The lifestyles that they enjoy were paid for with Afrikan blood, sweat, and tears. Today's slaves threaten and berate their own people the moment that they open their stereotypically gold-plated mouths. Worse still are the rappers who hold themselves out as intellectuals. They remind us of Damon Wayans' incarcerated character

---

5   The mentality spawned after the Black Pride/Civil Rights Movement and promoted by modern hip hop entertainers.

on *In Living Color*. We all remember the brother who seemed to have read the whole dictionary but didn't understand a single word. Gangsta rap paves the way for slavery's return by undermining the authority of our ancestors. Instead of singing the praises of Thurgood Marshall or Ruby Dee, slave rappers glorify Noriega and various characters from the Mafia. The language that these rappers use sounds as if it comes from a Mafia movie. *Spray dem niggas. Chop dem niggas down. Black people are not worth being rapped about unless they are being shot or swinging from a stripper's pole.* Rap lyrics clearly tell the world that Black people are subhuman. Why should anyone respect Afrikan people when we give awards to people who rap about how violent, lazy, ignorant and immoral we are? How can we respect those Black men and women who walked through the hottest parts of Alabama summer so that we could ride? How can we appreciate the sacrifices of our Black ancestors when Blackness has come to mean being a degenerate?

Afrikan Americans who were born before the Post-pride era know ancestral reverence very well. Any one of us will tell you that we dared not disrespect our elders. It didn't matter whether they were relatives, teachers, or neighbors. We valued the stories that older people told. We sought their advice all the time. When we decided to go against their advice and things went wrong, our elders were there to remind us that we wouldn't be in that predicament if we had listened to them in the first place. Today our neighborhoods and schools are overrun with uncultured, violent young people who haven't the slightest bit of home training. They never learned to revere their parents and therefore cannot respect any adult. Their parents are modern day slaves. They give their children over to Massa. They allow their children to watch the soul-withering filth on MTV and BET. They encourage their children to act like slaves by dressing them like brain-dead rappers. In 1971, if a young Black child started gyrating her hips and singing, "Lick it like a lollipop", her mother would have clobbered her. She would have been reminded that she was "not grown". But many Black mothers today find this type of behavior "cute".

Of course the parents find it "cute". They barely have any sense themselves! One of the most glaring tragedies of the modern slave era is the reversal of roles within the Black community. Instead of the young people looking up to their elders, we have adults breaking their necks to imitate 20 year-old rappers and R&B singers! It is nothing short of a travesty when we see brothers in their forties sagging and wearing do-rags. Jesse Jackson is a prime example. He went from marching alongside Dr. King in the 1960's to being just another "baby daddy" today. These so-called Black artists are pied pipers leading elders and young folks down a path of degradation and hatred of self. This is how the strategies in the "Willie Lynch" letter perpetuate themselves. Our young people have no idea what constitutes proper or even normal behavior. Where would they learn that? Their parents are little more than large children themselves. When they turn on their televisions and radios, they see nothing but rich slaves encouraging them to get with the program. This is about much more than a vicious cycle designed to keep Black people down. Who really benefits from these continued attacks on our own culture?

Anyone who says that rap has always been anti-ancestral is both deaf and blind. Indeed, *Rapper's Delight*[6] begins with an ice-cold Afrikan drum routine. Run DMC praise Harriet Tubman for

---

6   Sugar Hill Gang, 1979.

her bravery in *Proud to Be Black*. Chuck D. (Public Enemy) makes numerous references to Black figures such as Huey Newton and Malcolm X. MC Lyte's *Cappuccino* (1989) warned us of the dangers of drug abuse and the disintegration of the Black family. In 1990, X-Clan opened *The Ways of the Scales* with recitations from ancient Kemetic Scripture. And we were blessed with eloquent reminders of our responsibility to educate ourselves and nurture our Afrikan spirits from Rakim. His album *18ᵗʰ Letter: Book of Life* remains a beacon to young Afrikan people seeking knowledge of self to this day. These are just a few examples. Were we to list all of the ways in which Old School rap praised the artistry and perseverance of our forefathers, we would fill several chapters. At present, there are very few artists that display ancestral reverence in their lyrics or in the way they present themselves. Pharoahe Monche's remake of Public Enemy's *Welcome to the Terrordome* (featuring Chuck D.) was a breath of fresh air. We were pleased to see a rapper from the latter generation helping to preserve the wisdom of Old School hip hop. Groups like Zion I also struggle against the mainstream to keep our ancestral traditions alive.

Self-Preservation

Every society seeks to promote and protect its welfare. This can mean education, advances in medicine, agricultural innovations, or even a show of military strength to enforce the society's political and geographical boundaries. Our people in the Congo organized a 5-nation coalition opposing the slave trade. They won victory after victory over the Portuguese and rescued many communities from the horrors of captivity. They were not fighting out of racial hatred. They knew that unspeakable torments awaited us in the West. These Afrikans sought to preserve their families and their way of life. One well-known modern example of self-preservation can be found in France. The French insist that all advertising in their country must be in the French language. Words like "cool" and "ain't" are very popular in Europe. Advertisers find that they make more sales when they throw a few American or Ebonics expressions in their commercials. The French government imposes a fine on marketers for every English word that they use. This applies to television, radio, and billboards. Some people interpret this to be just another instance of French snobbery. In reality, it is nothing more than self-preservation. If the French continue to adopt English words and slang, it will erode their understanding and use of their own language. Then it will be as difficult to find a person in France who speaks proper French as it is to find an American who speaks proper English. The quality of their literature and cinema will decline. There is nothing wrong with people in France saying, "This is France. Speak French!" West Afrikan groups used secret societies as a way of preserving their culture and quality of life. The members of these clandestine organizations were entrusted with the knowledge necessary to protect the community. They know the locations of certain herbs in the forests that can be used as medicine. They know where large caches of weapons and other valuable items are hidden. The Komo of Mali is a secret society. Very little is known about them to this day. This is why it is outrageous to see Black college students submitting to humiliating initiation rites just so that they can wear Greek letters on their sweaters. If they had knowledge of self, they would know that our people had secret societies before Greece ever existed. Denying one's Blackness and calling oneself a "Greek" preserves European society, not ours. Five minutes in Greece would show them just how "Greek" they really are! Self-preservation is the reason that so little is known today about the particulars of many sacred Kemetic (Egyptian) ceremonies. There are religious texts that speak about "transforming into a falcon" and references to "magic rings" throughout the material that has been recovered by archeologists. Europeans take this to mean that Afrikans are superstitious and gullible. On the contrary, the texts are purposefully riddled with obscurities and metaphors to prevent the transmission of sacred knowledge to outsiders. Examples of self-preservation among Afrikan Americans would fill an entire encyclopedia. It is the reason we practice communalism. We participated in "sit-ins" and were brutalized by savage policemen because we wanted to survive. The racist laws of America were killing us. Society had to be forced to change so that we could live.

Hip Hop's Assault on the Afrikan Identity

The slave trade in West Afrika did not begin overnight. It took decades to string together a network of traders and catchers. Roads had to be carved through the forests. Watering stations had to be set up in the desert. But before any of this could take place, the Afrikan identity had to be destroyed. Our ancestors had to lose all faith in the legitimacy of Black authority. The European answer for ancestral reverence was ministers and priests. Converts to Christianity obeyed their Catholic "fathers" to the letter. They lost all respect for their own priests and medicine men. At one time, disputes were settled by local chiefs and religious counselors. After digesting the Bible (as explained to them by Caucasian missionaries), they began to take all of their problems to White people.

The authority of the Black man waned. Having gained the confidence of Afrikan people, the Europeans then challenged the jurisdiction of the Kings and Queens. They stirred up violent conflicts between different provinces, arming each side with guns from Europe. The King's army was spread thin as it tried to put down theses civil wars. Before anyone realized it, the whole country was surrounded and overrun with European soldiers. As for self-preservation, Europeans brought guns and liquor. To this day, many poor Black people in America live in neighborhoods where there are liquor stores on every corner and a gun in every pocket.

"Willie Lynch's" program is only effective in the absence of the Afrikan identity. As long as our ancestors knew who they were, they were safe. Afrikans never bothered with proselytizing or forcing other Afrikans to adopt their religious beliefs. This produced an atmosphere of spiritual freedom. We were free to ponder the universe from a perspective that was culturally and philosophically familiar. Once we began to judge ourselves by European standards, the Europeans became the masters of our reality. It is important to point out that Islam offered us no refuge from the war on our identity. The Quran permits selling "non-believers" into bondage. "Non-believers" applies to every one of our ancestors because they practiced traditional Afrikan religions instead of Islam. Afrika became a smorgasbord of slaves as Blacks who had converted to Islam grew rich and fat off of the suffering of millions of their own neighbors and even relatives. Nigerian Muslims were extremely eager to enter into business with the Europeans. 40% of Afrikan Americans have origins in Nigeria because the Muslims and Christians there sold off their own people left and right. Many of our ancestors found themselves being beaten and raped in the South with the full sanction of both Christianity and Islam. Many Black people still believe that all our ancestors had to do was convert to Islam and they would be let go. If that was true, there never would have been a single Black slave in Saudi Arabia, Sudan, or Yemen! Every one of us would at least claim to convert to Islam if it meant getting our freedom back. On the contrary, Afrikan people were treated with the same kind of cruelty in Islamic countries as in the American South. The oppressor's hatred of Blackness guaranteed that they would always be enslaved no matter what religion they practiced.

Rappers attack the Afrikan identity in a similar fashion. According to today's slaves, we are not the proud human beings that would rather walk in the cold than be somebody's nigger on the back of the bus. Black women and children are not worth protecting. No, we are all a bunch of niggas and motherfuckers. Two rationalizations are given when we are asked why we use the word "nigga" to describe our people. The first excuse is a feeble attempt at reverse psychology. Some Black people contend that using the word takes the power out of it. After all, how can someone insult us by calling us a name that we already call ourselves? The "logic" behind this foolishness is indeed weak. Since when did using something take the power out of it? Does using drugs make them less addictive? The "power" argument is nothing but New Age cowardice. If we can't beat them, why not join them? If we cannot stop others from using the word, why not hurl this hate-filled epithet at our brothers, sisters, and even our own children? Why not just put out our wrists and allow them to shackle us in self-hatred? It is an admission of weakness and helplessness. It is a celebration of more than 400 years of abuse and genocide against the Afrikan race. Apparently these lost brothers and sisters wish to keep the traditions of the plantation alive. The second excuse given for the use of the word "nigga" is that it doesn't mean the same thing when used by Black people as it does when other races use it. Therefore, they will answer to the name that our captor hissed between his clenched teeth as he raped Black women. They will address our people on the streets with the word that was screamed in our ears as the whip cut our flesh, as we dangled by our throats from blood-soaked trees. Suddenly, according to these slaves, it means something different now. And does it really? Statistics reveal that 49% of all homicides in the United States are Black people[7]. Over the last 25 years, other Blacks murdered 94% of all Black victims in the US. When these slaves rap about killing "niggas", to whom are they referring?

Niggas are described as irrational, immature and extremely violent with an animalistic type of sexuality. Hip hop lyrics depict niggas fighting, using and selling narcotics, and abandoning their children. Niggas are predatory; lurking in the shadows, waiting to "catch a nigga slippin'" so they can rob him. Niggas are also expendable. Rappers are very specific. They do not brag about all of the *men* that they have robbed and murdered. They brag about all the *niggas* that they have killed. Afrikan people celebrate this mentality by laughing, rapping along, and bouncing to the beat. It is most disturbing. At this point, the slaves among us will begin to grumble. They will offer the sorry argument that the word "nigga" no longer only applies to Black people. They will claim that it now carries some universal-urban connotation that has more to do with popular culture than race or history. Indeed, Afrikans are not the only people to refer to themselves and their people as niggas.

---

7   US Department of Justice: 2003 Criminal Victimization Survey.

There are Latinos, Asians, and Caucasians who identify themselves this way. Some feel that they embody the spirit of the urban struggle. Others simply do it because it's fashionable. As for the first group, any association between the word "nigga" and non-Black people is both voluntary and imaginary. Not one of them has the faintest idea about what being a nigga means. Not one of them has ancestors who went through the Middle Passage! Not one of them has an ancestor who was hung or felt the lash ripping their skin. When signs were posted that read *NIGGER, DON'T LET THE SUN SET ON YOU IN THIS TOWN*, were Asians and Whites the intended target? When have Caucasians ever been left on the steps of segregated hospitals to die or denied all opportunities for education? They know nothing of our struggle. How convenient it is to step under the umbrella of the word "nigga" at this stage in the game. It truly is heart-wrenching to consider how these "niggas" have suffered: the long applications they had to fill out in order to take advantage of programs such as Affirmative Action that Black people gave up our lives to put into place. And it must be nothing short of torment for them to stand in the long lines at the bank in order to cash checks received for imitating or otherwise exploiting our culture. Yet it was Black people who set the stage for this insanity. Calling each other niggas, hoes, and motherfuckers taught non-Blacks that we care nothing for one another. They are merely following our example. We must understand that we are never simply being watched. We are always being *studied.* The world studies Black people carefully and abuses or exploits us to the extent that their findings indicate are possible. Our rejection of the Civil Rights Era values teaches the world that our heritage and culture mean nothing to us. How could it, when we use it solely for the purposes of making money and dehumanizing our own people?

Not only have we allowed the madness in mainstream hip pop to destroy our community, but it has eroded the respect that existed between us and other races as well. The idea that calling each other niggas and hoes has somehow united the younger generations is a fallacy. Other races listening to hip pop does not equal a welcome into their culture. On the contrary, they are being welcomed into ours! Racist people eat Chinese and Mexican food. It does not mean that they love the Chinese or the Mexicans. They just love the food! In January of 1999, a Black student at Skyline High School was attacked by an Asian student with a crowbar. In 2004, violence between Blacks and Latinos left 57 injured at Wilma Amina Carter High School in Rialto, California. The majority of the injured students were Black. The same was true in Fremont, California, where 150 students were injured in a brawl. Where Blacks and Latinos once benefited from mutual goals and understandings, there is now separation and bloodshed. Have the Latinos changed into a new kind of people? Absolutely not. Black men have changed into niggas. We have been relentless in the destruction of our image. Just as James Brown's Say It Loud moved non-Blacks to recognition of our uniqueness and strength, rap music teaches non-Blacks to treat us like weak niggas.

Niggas are the creation of murderous, thieving, child-molesting slave owners. Their history begins with their people in chains. The nigga was kept in chains, beaten, hung, molested, abused. The nigga is poor and lives in the ghetto, or he is rich and lives on a mental plantation. He is weak, hunted, and afraid, which in turn makes him desperate, wild, and violent. He has no honor. He is not to be trusted. He lies. He steals. This type of identification has weakened Black men. Our men have become frightened, desperate, and sissified. Niggas have never held control over any country. They have no language save those of their oppressors. They have no religion except those which supported the doctrine of slavery and upheld the system in which Black children were repeatedly molested, our women ravaged, and our men tortured and murdered. Afrikans, on the other hand, have a long and glorious history. We comprise a wide range of cultures and religions. We are the ones who brought the gift of humanity. We are the sons and daughters of ancient Kemet, Punt, Kush/Nubia, Shona, and Timbuktu. Afrikans speak over two thousand languages. Afrika serves as a treasure trove of knowledge, wisdom, and experience. We have our own heroes: Agaja Trudo, Imhotep, Askia Mohammed, Julius Nyere, Steven Biko, and countless others. We realize that our present condition is just a bump in the road. We know that we are equipped for the challenge of the coming years. All that is necessary is that we practice "iwe pele" (good character) as the Ifa among us say, or that we keep "livin' right", as say the brothers and sisters in the United States.

What's wrong with calling ourselves niggas, hoes, and thugs? What effects does it have on our ideas and behavior? In 1937, Dr. Konrad Lorenz of Austria performed a series of experiments with newly hatched ducklings and goslings. He found that the birds were capable of strange behavior if exposed to unusual influences during their impressionable stage (the first few hours after hatching). If the young birds were exposed to humans instead of other birds, they became socially bonded to people. They would even try to mate with humans when they became sexually mature. Lorenz found that infant animals do not naturally recognize their own kind and will adopt some of the behaviors of whatever they were exposed to during the impressionable stage[8]. Lorenz' study was one of many that proved time after time that sense of identity directly influences behavior. If a bird identifies with a human being, it adopts human behaviors. Identity works the same way in the human mind. We adopt the behaviors of those with whom we identify.

If rap music so offends our Afrikan sensibilities, wouldn't it be better to just stop listening to it? It would not matter if we did. One does not have to listen to rap music to be affected by the mentality that it encourages. The children at Malcolm X Academy in San Francisco, California acted out a funeral at lunchtime for a young Black girl who found out that her father had been shot as soon as she arrived at school that day. In 2001, Teachers in the Hunter's Point district asked Mayor Willie Brown and the Board of Education for more resources-counselors and learning materials- to help them deal with all of the violence and tragedy that surrounds Black children's lives. Our young brother, Lee Smith Jr. of San Diego, California, was merely sitting at a bus stop when a drive-by shooting ended his life (2004). He died in surgery at the age of 16. He was not listening to rap music. He was sitting and talking with four friends. Little 12 year-old Delarrian Davis of Missouri was murdered by an ignorant, modern day slave in October of 2008. Was he listening to rap music? No, he was doing his homework! The modern day slave that killed him, however, was living out the lyrics of a typical rap song as he carried out the drive-by shooting. We do not have to listen to rap music to be carjacked or to be the victims of home invasions. The business owners in New York, New Orleans, and Los Angeles who were forced to close their doors due to gang violence were

---

8   Hess, Eckhard and Petrovich, Slobodan: Imprinting. 1977.

not blasting rap music. The idea that we should just not listen or be concerned is of the slave mentality. It implies that what goes on in our communities is none of our business. Black people are concerned about the erosion of our beautiful culture. We will not simply turn off the radio or television and pretend that these problems do not exist.

Sambos (or Coons): The Enemy Within

Sambos (also known as "coons") are active and willing agents of "Willie Lynch's" policies. We take the name "Sambo" from Harriet Beecher Stowe's *Uncle Tom's Cabin*. Many Black people who have not read the book mistakenly refer to Uncle Tom as a traitor. In reality, Sambo and Quimbo were the self-hating slaves who were eager to demonstrate their loyalty to the Caucasians at the expense of their own people. Uncle Tom actually confronted the slave owner for raping a sister. One modern-day example of coonery is the short-lived *Chappelle Show*. Dave Chappelle happily called us all a bunch of niggas and bitches to delight his mainly White audience. Sambos are completely indoctrinated in the "Willie Lynch" program. For these wretched souls, it is much more than mere theory. Sambos truly believe that Black people are inferior to other races in every way. Sambos swell with pride and say, "My grandmother looked just like a White woman." They don't say, "My grandmother was a very pretty woman." That's not the point. The point was that she "looked White". The more features that a person has that are similar to those typically found among Caucasians, the more "beautiful" they are. Sambos believe that we are an ugly race. At their first opportunity, most Sambos (feminine:

Sambolines) latch onto a Caucasian mate. They don't find a mate based on compatibility, shared culture, interests, or goals. They choose their mates based on how unlike the "ugly" Negroes they look. Flava Flav's buffoonery on the reality show *Strange Love* is a prime example. For those of us who remember Flav's days as a pro-Afrikan, militant member of Public Enemy, it was downright scandalous. The program went on for weeks. In every episode, Flava Flav nearly breaks his neck trying to win the affection of a thousand year old mummy. The woman clearly had been dried and/or pickled centuries ago. The show was little more than an enactment of long-standing racist fantasies about the Black man's unquenchable lust for Caucasian women. For a Sambo, any Caucasian woman is better than a sister. Any Hispanic man is better than a brother, no matter what his circumstances are. The Sambo is not so much running towards the Caucasian race as he (or she) is running away from his own Blackness. They are running away from their own wide noses and kinky hair. They are desperate to escape the shame of their enslaved past. Their complete ignorance of their own history has made them nameless. Instead of accepting responsibility for educating themselves, they latch onto the histories of other people. They want to be on the "winning team". Ultimately, the relationships with their non-Afrikan partners are just as dysfunctional as those they attempted to have with members of our race.

Through the eyes of a Sambo, all Black people are poor, uneducated, frightened and trivial. We are imprisoned in our own small minds. For them, that is where we belong. They intend to see to it that we stay there. Sambos have an intense hatred for the fortune or happiness of other Black people.

Who do those niggas think they are? Sambos hate successful Afrikans because it upsets Massa Willie's universe. *That's not how it's supposed to be! You ain't supposed to own no house, nigga. You ain't got no business in college. Oh, you think you're getting' a promotion, nigga? Wait 'til I get in the boss' ear.* Oh yes! The Sambo will snitch, lie, and even set other Black people up on the job rather than see us enjoy the fruits of our own labor. The Sambo seeks a pat on the head from Massa Willie like the hind-end-sniffing dog that he is. He has a pathetic need to be special, more beloved by Massa than the rest of the Negroes. Even when Massa is being cruel, Sambos continue to seek their favor. Sambos continued to support a White entertainer after the discovery of this artist's racist recordings. The lyrics in these recordings explicitly state that "Black girls are no good" and that "White girls are the best". This sort of trash appeals to Sambos because it gives voice to their extreme hatred of all things Afrikan. Sambos in prison will pick fights with or otherwise set up inmates that are nearing their release date. These Sambos do not receive anything at all for having caused the other inmate to miss his release date. They do it for the sheer thrill of inflicting hurt on their own kind. Sambos can be found everywhere. They slither around in the offices where we work, wearing a path on the carpet to the supervisor's office where they sing like canaries about every word their Black co-workers utter. They lurk in the government, where they vote to cancel the very programs that helped them reach their educational goals, such as Affirmative Action. They denounce any Afrikan organization that wishes to do more than marching and singing even though they would not be able to walk through the doors of the Capitol Building had it not been for the fire that these "militants" lit under the government's feet. They are so busy trying to assure Massa that they are not "one of the troublemakers" that they put themselves exactly where they were brought here to be- completely under the thumb of their oppressors. Do not attempt to treat or cure Sambo Syndrome. Sambos are legendary backstabbers and chronic liars. They worship Europeans. We mustn't be foolish enough to believe that we can convince anyone to betray their god.

The mainstream rap circuit is brimming with Sambos. Rappers go to ridiculous lengths to make it seem that they are outside of the law, but are they really? Since when did Western nations care about the loss of Black life? Thugs have guns in the trunk, but on whom do they turn these weapons? *Not you, Massa! I'm killin them niggas.* They have incredible amounts of money, but what happens to it? *I made all this money, but I'm giving it right back to you, Massa. I loves you, Massa. Black women are hoes. Want to see? I'll make them bend over and "twerk" something for the entire world. That's how low our women can go.* Of course the world loves mainstream rap! It provides them an opportunity that the Civil Rights Era had deprived them of- the chance to call us niggas and laugh right to our faces. It keeps our men divided and weak. The post-Pride mentality makes us *all* easy to control. It entices outsiders to abuse Black people. What are we going to do? Why *wouldn't* our votes be thrown out in 2000? *Niggas* weren't supposed to be voting in this country in the first place! Why *wouldn't* the police murder, taser, and chain up Black children as young as 5 years old? What are Black people going to do about it? The answer is obvious. We have already told the world what we will do. While all of these things have been going on in our communities, we have been rapping about murdering one another, selling drugs, and pimping our sisters. *That* is what the hip pop contingent will do. This type of music is relentlessly marketed towards our children. Embracing the slave mindset at an early age assures that there will be plenty of Sambos in the future. They will pose no threat to the status quo. Their interests will be robbing, killing, and trafficking narcotics. They will dutifully rush into prison or their graves. They will be good slaves. This is infinitely more pleasing to Massa than the antics of those troublemaking "Afrikan" Blacks, who are constantly poking their noses into history, mathematics, science, medicine, and all other places we "don't belong".

The erosion of the Afrikan identity in rap music cuts rap off from its cultural base. It turns our own art into a weapon against us. There are people in Cambodia and Bosnia who have never seen an Afrikan person but who still "know" that we are to be called niggas. They "know" that our women are to be called "bitches" and that Black women are perpetually available for sex. They have been taught by our own Afrikan brothers and sisters that we are a nation of "baby mamas" and "baby daddies" who possess such a deep sense of self-hatred that we are unable to speak without cursing our entire race. Gangsta rap has taught the world that we are just what they always accused us of being. In the minds of many, it justifies every horrible act that has been committed against our people. We were just going to murder each other anyway, so what difference does it make? It justifies the brutalization of our women. They're just hoes anyway, so what was wrong with wrestling our women down behind the barns when we were captives? What's wrong with groping the Black female co-worker in modern times? That Black artists would choose to celebrate abasement instead of triumph and glory is not only unfortunate, but foolish indeed. It squanders all of the intelligence and labor that went into laying the musical foundations of rap. East Coast rappers know that they are heirs to the cosmic vision of George Clinton, the grace of Patti Austin, and the strength of Stephanie Mills. Midwestern rappers are well acquainted with the flawless delivery of Howard Hewett and Anita Baker's soulful expression. Midwest rappers also know that they walk in the footsteps of George Benson, one of the most innovate and talented musicians of all time. Hip pop artists from the South realize that they are part of a great legacy. Al Green, Lionel Richie, Ray Charles, and a host of other Black entertainers shaped the musical traditions that they enjoy today. Southern rappers are also the children of the Civil Rights Era, which was particularly strong in Alabama, Georgia, Mississippi, and Arkansas. The same can be said of West Coast rappers. The cities of Oakland, San Francisco, San Jose, and Los Angeles were bastions of Black Pride for decades. It cannot be argued that these rappers have never heard of these artists. They sample their music left and right. Post-Pride culture seeks to destroy the artistic and social advances that brought rap into existence in the first place.

Culture is simply a vehicle for navigating through life. Art, music, cuisine, and even leisure activities such as sports are all geared towards the survival of the clan. Rap no longer serves this purpose. It focuses on humiliating, robbing, poisoning and killing our own people. Mainstream rap is geared toward genocide. Claiming our heritage allows us to own the gifts that we brought to this world: music, science, mathematics, athleticism, and a rich literary tradition. Having a solid understanding of our true identity allows us to aspire to higher stations in life. Embracing the true values of our people means embracing education, respecting our bodies, and doing for self and kind. It gives us a chance to at last claim our piece of the pie that the ancestors baked. As our brother Paul Robeson told the House Un-American Activities Committee in 1956, "My father was a slave and my people built this country, and I'm going to stay right here and have a part of it." Revering our heritage does not mean blindly accepting any practice that is considered "Afrikan". Afrikan cultures are man-made institutions and have flaws like every other man-made thing. This is one of the greatest dangers of the hip hop mentality. As Traditionalists, Christians and Muslims, we recognize the Universal Laws. We have no doubt that we exist in a friendly and helpful universe. The flaws in our culture (and indeed, our personal lives) are only there to reveal areas in which greater inner and outer work is needed. We understand the Law of Attraction and that beauty attracts Beauty. The slave mind, however, preaches about an evil universe that is ruled by an uncaring and distant God. Today's minstrels teach that we can only reach salvation by destroying our own people. This is oceans apart from our original nature. We cannot make significant progress until we know who we truly are. We are not the people depicted in slave rap lyrics. Our women are not the sleazy savages described in today's poor excuse for R&B. The true story of the modern era has not yet been told. The first step towards healing ourselves is removing the mask.

CHAPTER TWO

Shameless Shorties: The New Female Slaves

"Where there is no shame, there is no honor."
—Ethiopian proverb

The Post-Pride mentality has profound implications on the lives of Afrikan women today. Their health, finances, educational opportunities and spiritual development hang in the balance as a result of their active (albeit usually unwitting) participation in the cycle of degradation that is the Willie Lynch program. Whether we live in London or Sao Paolo, we should be celebrating the Black woman. We should be teaching and encouraging her to celebrate herself. The single Afrikan mother has become an archetype. Whenever we talk about Black women, her image comes to mind. It is within this picture of the Black woman that we most easily recognize her strength and the depth of her sacrifices. She is the one who drags herself out of bed on cold mornings to go to a job where she is underpaid and underappreciated. The single mother is the one who plays the dual role of Mama and Daddy. She is also the family doctor, chauffeur, cook, maid, spiritual advisor, hairdresser and protector. Through her many thankless roles, she commits thousands of acts of kindness and generosity and secures a beautiful spiritual return for all her years of faithful service. We must not neglect to also celebrate the Afrikan wife. The Black woman is a shrewd and capable partner, not only in times of prosperity but through the tough times as well.

The Post-pride woman offers no evidence that she considers herself the picture of selfless generosity and spirituality. The scope of her consciousness is severely limited. Stripped of her natural identity through her identification as both a "nigga" and a "bitch", she can only hope for things that are possible for niggas and bitches. Black women simply cannot afford to identify this way. The world does not make allowances for people who have been misled or brainwashed. Learning their lesson is the only thing that will lift the weight of ignorance from their backs. Science, medicine and business are all areas in which Black women from the Post-Pride generation are sorely underrepresented. This is not because they are incapable of excelling in these fields. We have no idea of exactly what they are capable of because education is not high on the Post-Pride generation's list of priorities. They do not suffer from a lack of role models. Many Black women enjoy successful careers in science. Some are visionaries. Others are pioneers. Diane Jordan, the founding director of the Human Genome Project at Howard University in Washington, DC, was the first Afrikan American woman to graduate with a doctorate in Genetics in 1972. She uses the data collected to study diseases such as diabetes that affect Afrikan people disproportionately in the United States and Caribbean. Claudia Alexander worked as a science coordinator for the plasma wave instrument mounted on the Galileo spacecraft. She was later promoted to Project Manager for the entire Galileo Mission[9]. Dr. Sonya Summerour Clemmons holds an MBA as well as a PhD in Biomedical Engineering. She currently works in the field of biomedical products and devices, making a vast contribution to the improved condition of ill and injured people all over the world. But the mentality espoused by women and girls in today's R&B

9   Galileo was a spacecraft mission launched in 1989 to study Jupiter and its satellites.

is vacuous and limited. Hip hop culture teaches Black women to use their brains for trifling and trivial pursuits. In this way, it robs them of all hope. Black women will never rise above the level of their own self-image. Bitches and hoes have no place in college or at the head of a legitimate corporation. They have no patience for learning anything that does not help them find a man to buy them shiny things. Many sisters complain that no matter where they go they cannot find a decent man, a good job, or any measure of true happiness. This is because everywhere they go, they bring *themselves*. They believe that they are bitches and hoes. They attract men who think of them this way and treat them accordingly. Even finding a man with deep pockets does not abate their misery. What the Post-pride woman wants most is to completely possess a man, but the rules of ghetto mentality clearly state that no woman can hope to have a man all to herself. If she wants to be down- if she wants to be a playa in the game- she must accept indiscretions on the part of her man without complaint. These lost sisters actually accept a man's excuse that she "knew what this about when she first got with him". This only makes her desire to possess him stronger. Instead of growing a spine and heading for fairer pastures, she turns her rage and disappointment on herself, her children, and on her Black sisters. What unhappy days await the sister who becomes tangled up with a self-hating Samboline!

A woman that cherishes the materialistic ideals of the Post-Pride generation is doomed to fail. She is forever looking outside of herself and her culture for happiness. Her focus is on clothing, shoes and handbags. No matter how expensive her handbag is today, tomorrow there will be a more glamorous and expensive purse. Then what will she do? No matter how large her wardrobe, she will never be able to collect every "cute" piece of clothing in the world. No matter how expensive her manicure or how rare her perfume, there will always be a bigger and better new thing. The Post-Pride woman's life is one long and ridiculous competition with all her Black sisters. She is insecure. She desperately needs to find at least one area in life where she can say that she is better than other Afrikan women. She is trifling and petty.

Hateraid: The Post-Pride Woman's Favorite Drink

In 1858, Harriet Tubman was nearly captured during the rescue of an enslaved brother known as "Nalle". They were both detained by the police, who instantly began to beat and verbally abuse our beloved Mother. The Troy *Daily Times* reported that "colored women" rushed into battle, fighting off the entire squad of police officers. Every time the thieving, inbred cops managed to get their hands on Nalle, he was pulled away by the crowd of knife and skillet-wielding sisters. At one point, the police seemed to have gained the upper hand. They succeeded in dragging Mother Harriet and her "passenger" to the steps of the local courthouse. Seeing their beloved Mother Harriet being seized and roughed up by the officers only fueled their determination to help her escape. They fired off a steady barrage of rocks and chunks of cement. The officers were armed, but they did not have the opportunity to shoot into the crowd. They only had time to try to seek cover. Those who did not manage to shelter themselves suffered serious (fatal, for some) head injuries. The defeated and bloody cops were forced to let go of Harriet and her passenger.

One would imagine that sisters today would present a united front. After all, it was the coordination and cooperation of Black women that freed us from bondage. One would think that the Black woman would learn that solidarity with her sisters leads to success. This is not the case with Sambolines. The slave mindset renders Black women unable to do anything except perpetuate the Willie Lynch program. Although it is painfully apparent in Black male-female relationships, this sickness taints the relationships between our sisters as well. The modern she-slave has absolutely no respect for herself or her womanhood. It is impossible for her to respect other Black women. She sees them through the eyes of 300 years of protracted slavery and internalized racism. Other Black women are "bitches" and "hoes". Her job is to keep other Black women down. She's doing Massa's job for him. Other Black women will not get promotions, decent jobs or a decent man on *her* watch! No matter how attractive she appears on the outside, she is empty inside. She is miserable and looking for company.

One of the most dangerous manifestations of this petty, cowardly mindset is the she-slave's love of breaking up Black families. The sighting of a well-mannered brother spending time with his children should fill us with pride and hope about the next generation of fathers. But this is not the case with the she-slave! When she sees a responsible brother with his children, she instantly begins to spin her web. She creates an entire catalogue of reasons why she is "better for him than that bitch" and why he "needs to be with" her. If she wasn't a weak and ignorant slave, she would have enough self-esteem not to want some other woman's leftovers. Even female cockroaches don't scheme and fight over males! The modern she-slave uses sex, lies, and other traps to destroy Black families. Because she denies her heritage and is too weak and foolish to connect with her true self, the thought of other Black women, men, and children living in a happy family fills her with rage. She acts as her sister's overseer. Any attempt on the good sister's part to improve her life is considered insolence. She must be knocked down a peg or two. The she-slave is the perfect fool for the job. The fact that children might be separated from their fathers means nothing to her. *Them little niggas don't need no daddy no way. They probably ain't even his.* We are thoroughly sickened when we compare their behavior to that of captive sisters who fought without regard for their personal safety to help one another keep their families together on the plantations. We even witness this kind of behavior from Black mothers. *That baby ain't my grandchild!* She goes on talk shows and stoops to every low form of behavior, yelling *That bitch is lying on my son. She's a hoe!* It never occurs to them to teach their sons the consequences of unprotected sex. They never give their son the option of either paying for paternity tests (to clear up the matter once and for all) or moving out of Mama's house. Sambolines can only raise Sambos. They can be very creative when it comes to making excuses for their sons. The son becomes so dependent on his mother's excuses that he becomes an excuse himself. He is an excuse for a man and a poor one at that.

The she-slave has another powerful weapon in her war against the Afrikan family. She abuses her friendship with and influence over other sisters to turn them against the men in their lives. With little or no evidence, the she-slave suggests to her girlfriends that her man is being unfaithful. If the sister mentions having the slightest difficulty with her man, the Samboline inevitably replies, *Girl you should leave that nigga alone. He ain't no good, girl.* Meanwhile she is planning to seduce or otherwise snare the good sister's man. If the woman is foolish enough to listen to the she-slave, her family is destroyed. The slave is overjoyed. The man is gone. His authority in the home is no more. The woman and her children are miserable. And the she-slave has had the pleasure of watching it all unfold. In addition, she now has access to the discarded man for sex or mere bragging rights. The she-slave is proud of her accomplishments.

Many unsuspecting Afrikan men also become pawns in the she-slaves' pitiful games. Far too many brothers believe that they are in healthy, progressive relationships when the truth is that they are tools in a Samboline competition. A she-slave has no use for a good Black man. She views his righteousness as a threat. In her world, all Black men are trifling, violent, and ignorant. Their materialism and greed are merely symptoms of an agonizing emptiness that will never be filled. The Samboline attempts to fill this void by competing with like-minded she-slaves over who can get men to spend the most money on them. She has no patience for men that she foolishly labels "cheap". She cannot show her friends that her boyfriend or husband made dinner last night. No one can see that her man passed on a chance to go out with his friends and stayed at home with her. She needs something on her wrist or around her neck so that she can *show them other hoes* that she is better than they are. The she-slave demands expensive "tokens" of her man's affection. Unwise brothers empty their wallets in vain attempts at winning her favor. When the money dries up, she latches onto the next fool with deep pockets. This sort of competition among our sisters is a waste of time. The trinkets that they receive from their hapless suitors may be shiny, but a trip to any pawn shop will quickly reveal that they have very little cash value. The cars are repossessed-either by the man himself or the car dealer. In the end, the Samboline finds that she has whored herself out for two or three hundred dollars worth of inferior gold and flawed gemstones. This is what happens when Black women allow the uncultured, herpes-laden females of mainstream rap and R&B to dictate their notion of womanhood. Those of us who have retained our Afrikan minds are grateful for artists such as India Arie and Alicia Keys who consistently remind our women that they need not degrade themselves in order to be "somebody". We are abuzz whenever Teedra Moses, Erykah Badu or Liv Warfield releases a new CD. These types of performers give us hope that R&B will return to its roots.

"Gittin' Loud": The Samboline's Version of Diplomacy

The ranges and types of roles offered to Black people have changed dramatically over the last 50 years. Black men are no longer restricted to playing butlers, pimps, and rapists on screen. Black women have gone from playing silent maids to owning their own production studios. But one image of the Black woman has survived all of the positive changes in Hollywood. The loud, disrespectful, irrepressible, sassy-mouthed Black woman continues to haunt us to this day. The vast majority of today's female rappers fall into this category. So do most of the female characters in popular sitcoms. The ratchet-mouthed Black woman is an open enemy of diplomacy. She teaches our young sisters by example that the only way to solve a problem is by getting loud, using filthy language, and refusing to compromise. The slightest provocation is enough to send her on a rampage. From her warped perspective, if the person she has yelled at appears to back down, she has won. She foolishly carries on this way in the workplace. Whenever a co-worker or superior assigns her a new task, she rants and raves and informs everyone within earshot about what she is "not going to do". The offended party often retreats without immediate retaliation, and so the Samboline believes that she has won. What she does not realize is that her supervisor returned to his or her office in order to post an advertisement in the local newspaper. As soon as the replacement has been hired and trained, the Samboline will be let go. She will accuse other Black women of having caused her a job, but the truth is that her own coon antics are to blame. Many Black children are also victims of this foolishness. It is truly embarrassing to witness the manner in which many Black women speak to their children in public. Sensible women expect that small children are going to misbehave from time to time. They may constantly need correcting. But instead of finding a civilized way to handle *a mere child*, the Samboline will call her own flesh and blood a barrage of niggas and motherfuckers. When we see a woman behaving this way, it is usually because her own mother taught her to do so. This is not a case of merely not knowing any better. The Samboline does not *want* to know any better! She is not going to spend her time learning anything except how to be the center of attention. Her poor children observe this and grow up behaving the same way. This is another one of the ways in which the slave mind is transmitted from mother to child.

Black women undo the work of the Civil Rights Era with their post-Pride antics. They spit upon the image built for them by the likes of Harriet Tubman, Sojourner Truth, Bessie and Sadie Delaney, and Rosa Parks. Our women of the post-Pride era have rejected the lessons wrought from the struggles of Tina Turner, Cicely Tyson, Mary J. Blige and Vanessa Williams. The very problems that the Post-pride woman claims are holding her down could have been solved years ago. All she has to do is stop running from herself and *learn from her history and her culture.* Instead, she uses our music-our splendid and unique gift from Afrika to orchestrate this insane death-style. She dishonors those who marched, who were dragged out of restaurants on their faces during sit-in protests, those who wrote and sang the songs that kept hearts afloat. She disgraces Afrika. She abuses the one thing that she could give us once we were snatched from her arms and dragged across the Atlantic Afrikan music. Our women have worn the post-Pride mask for so long that they do not recognize their real faces.

Bitches and Hoes: European Ideological Imports

We understand that the ideas underpinning the post-Pride contingent's estimation of the Black woman's worth did not originate in hip hop culture. These evil and misogynistic notions were first introduced to the world by European explorers. After being subjected to tremendous hospitality and generosity at the hands of Black people, European novelists, psychologists, anthropologists and historians busied themselves in a crazed campaign to dehumanize our people. They wrote volumes and volumes of books full of lies and their own dysfunctional fantasies. As far as the common people in Europe were concerned, these were the indisputable facts about Black people. It did not matter how bizarre or unlikely the accounts were. According to the accounts of these "authorities", we were another species, only distantly related to modern humans. We lacked all emotions save rage and lust. Black people were beasts. We were portrayed as having no more attachment to our spouses and families than a dog has for its mate. Our sisters were exotic, XXX-rated sexual beasts. Let us consider the words of Stuart Cloete, a South Afrikan colonizer (originally from France) in his novel *The African Giant*:

> "One is suddenly aware of the immense fecundity and sexuality of Africa. Many of the women were beautiful once you became used to African beauty. One could see why white men took them as housekeepers. They were all woman. They were, in a sense, without souls...They were bold and without innocence. They said with their dark eyes: We are women. You are a man. We know what you want."[10]

In his novel *The Sun Doctor*, Robert Shaw writes:

> "Certainly in Africa his needs of women had to some extent been met. Well, affection, yes passion, yes- nobody could smile more affectionately than Syoni- an exciting smile, a passionate smile, but not what you'd call sharing."[11]

This kind of misinformation was disseminated throughout the Western world to eliminate any feelings of empathy that could possibly lead to unrest in England, Germany, France, and the U.S. colonies. The accounts of our people were so appalling and outrageous that not only did the people abroad accept the brutal treatment of Blacks but they thought it was well-deserved. They had been taught that Afrikans were inhuman.

10   Cloete, Stuart: *The African Giant*. Collins London, 1957.
11   *The Sun Doctor*, Penguin Books, 1964.

No sane person would kick a defenseless, non-threatening human being. But one does not hesitate to stomp on a cockroach. European literature stripped us of our humanity so that we could be kicked, sold and tortured. Many Germans and British people thought that slavery was actually our salvation. It was better for us to be worked from one end of the day to the other, to have our women raped and our children molested than to be boiled alive in a big pot in Afrika as some sort of tribute to our bizarre gods. It was better to be beaten until permanent grooves crisscrossed our backs than to be swinging naked from the branches of trees in Afrika. This tactic is still employed by politicians and the media to this day and is known as "sensationalism". Its goal is influencing the emotions and reactions of the public. What else is modern R&B except the brazen celebration of the sensationalist claims of the oppressor? In the interest of fairness, we must note that the majority of Europe's population was illiterate. Most Europeans at the time had never read Cloete's books. But it was these types of ideas that fueled the government's propaganda. This notion that Black women are less than human allowed the common folk to beat and rape our sisters without experiencing the slightest pangs of pity or remorse. Today's slaves keep themselves in the dark about their own history and original nature, choosing instead to behave like animals. In this way, they keep the ideas of Cloete and his ilk alive.

None of the examples of today's trail-blazing Afrikan women will inspire the Post-pride woman to higher ideals and standards of living. Until she learns to identify with and love her Blackness, she is lost. What has Oprah to do with her if not for her Blackness (and therefore shared history)? What has Michelle Obama to do with her? What connection does she have to Makeda[12]? Who is Winnie Mandela if the post-Pride woman cannot recognize her as another sister caught up in the struggle? The rejection of Blackness and our history lies at the heart of the wretched Post-pride identity. It is for this reason that they are unable to see their own faces reflected in the eyes of the many people whose lives are shattered by their slave foolishness. They do not have any female Afrikan heroes. This is not only because they are unaware that such women exist, *but because their psychological shackles prevent them from even looking around to see if there are any.* In their minds, nothing is noble or beautiful about being Afrikan. In the absence of an appropriate model, they choose to emulate the she-slave that appears to be the top dog. This is usually the one with the loudest, foulest mouth. Black women perpetuate the rejection of the Afrikan identity in the subtlest of ways. It is not what they say, but what they do that expresses their denial of Blackness. When they are young, their mothers press and perm their hair. This is a habit that has been passed down since the days of slavery. Hundreds[13] of years later, these rituals of self-denial remain virtually unchanged among Afrikan people everywhere. Even on the Continent of Afrika, our sisters rush out to alter the grade of their hair. Our people have not gotten beyond the belief that there is something wrong with natural Black hair. Our sisters truly believe that they are not presentable unless they have hair that looks most unlike their own. When they observe Black R&B stars bleaching their hair and using camera tricks to lighten their skin on the covers of magazines, they learn that beautiful features are the opposite of Afrikan ones. They

---

12   Makeda is known as "Sheba" in the Bible and "Saba" in the Quran.

13   All colonized and/or enslaved Afrikan people became emancipated at different times, some as late as the 1990's.

become frozen. They are held fast by the chains of internalized racism. No Caucasian person need directly participate at this stage of the Willie Lynch program. For her, a dichotomy exists whereby Afrikan features are of the lowest rank and Caucasian features the highest. In truth, our hearts ache for these lost Afrikan souls. How long will they chose to carry the banner of slavery and self-hatred? What peace of mind awaits the sister that looks into the mirror and adores the Blackness that she sees! Her resplendent Afrikan locks, twists, plaits and puffs rival the majesty of the lion's mane and the delicate grace of peacock's tail. What a sense of power and freedom our sisters report when they no longer have to worry about running to the salon every few weeks to update their perm. They no longer have to constantly empty their pockets at their hairdresser or waste countless hours of their lives sitting in a stylist's chair. They feel none of the shame that they were taught as children and are surprised at how many more compliments they receive about their hair *now*.

Because their self-respect is dwindling, a shocking percentage of our women are failing to take care of themselves. According to the Center for Disease Control, 81% of Black women who were diagnosed with HIV in 2003 were infected through heterosexual contact[14]. This is another one of the dangers of the modern slave mentality. The Black woman's body is no longer a wondrous symbol of grace and fertility. It is no longer a temple. It is a moneymaker, an attention-getter. For too many sisters, it is piece of meat to be traded for something as paltry as a ride to the store or a value meal. Not only are these sisters putting themselves at risk for deadly diseases,

---

14   *HIV/AIDS Surveillance Report 2003 Volume 15*: US Department of Health and Human Services, Center for Disease Control.

but they are playing with our children's futures as well. In 2003, 69% of Afrikan children in the US were born to single mothers. This is in comparison with 25% for whites and 42% for Latinos. 55% of Black children were being raised in single parent homes. The figures were 23 and 31 percent for children of whites and Latinos respectively. Sisters no longer insist upon courtship. They find the whorish lifestyle described in rap and R&B lyrics "cute". But loss of control over her sexuality has never been cute for the Black woman! The historical (and continued) rape of our women all over the world has meant broken homes, humiliation, rage, misery and terror for millions. The idea that women of color were meant to suffer these ravages is tied up in the notion that they are less than women. What is less than a woman? A bitch? A hoe? The stereotypically hypersexual nature of modern female rappers is a slap in the face to our ancestors. That they refer to themselves as bitches and hoes only adds further insult to injury.

The New Afrikan Woman

For Black women, removing the mask means developing self-respect. Regardless of the claims of the Eurocentric feminists, the manner in which a woman presents herself has a direct influence upon the way she is perceived and treated. The feminists claim that a woman's manner of dress and speaking says nothing about her character. This is why we hear "You don't know me! You don't know nothin' about me!" from women that dress like strippers. Afrikan culture informs us that this is not true. Black women understand the concept of appropriate dress and presentation. If Michelle Obama had been a loud-talking, weave-wearing sister, her husband would not be in office today. In fact, if Mrs. Obama had *a single* tattoo, we would not have celebrated an Obama victory in 2008. The modern slave woman slams the door to her future shut with her ghetto appearance and foul behavior. She curses on her cell phone in public places, broadcasting intimate and inappropriate details of her life to everyone within earshot.

Black women that let go of the slave mentality gain the confidence necessary to prosper in the West. Many sisters are firmly anchored in the Afrikan traditions of marketing and entrepreneurship. They are not afraid to think outside of the box. They have no problem breaking away from the herd. Bitches and hoes make their living by celebrating the destruction of our people. Afrikan women provide for themselves and our community by using their intelligence and creativity. The results are impressive. Black women with bachelor's degrees earn slightly more than similarly educated white women. A white woman with a bachelor's degree typically earned nearly $37,800 in 2003, compared with $41,100 for a college-educated Black woman[15]. Though these statistics are encouraging, we must point out that a college education does not protect Black women from the ravages of the slave mind. It is important that we do not confuse formal education with knowledge of self! In the United States, 72% of Afrikan women who are business owners started their firms all on their own[16]. Where are the references to these facts in today's hip hop and R&B? 2 out of 5 Black-owned businesses in the United States are owned

---

15   US Census Bureau, March 2004.
16   Women Business Owners of Color: *New Accomplishments, Continuing Challenges.* Center for Women's Business Research, October 2002.

by sisters[17]. Educated sisters make important contributions to our quality of life. In 1975, Bath became the first Afrikan-American woman surgeon at the UCLA Medical Center and the first woman to be on the faculty of the UCLA Jules Stein Eye Institute. She is the founder and first president of the American Institute for the Prevention of Blindness. Patricia Bath was elected to Hunter College Hall of Fame in 1988 and elected as Howard University Pioneer in Academic Medicine in 1993. The laser instrument used for the popular eye surgery that is used all over the world was invented by a sister.

Rapper Sister Souljah has a degree from Rutgers University. She established (and financed) the Afrikan Youth Survival Program for children of homeless families. Severely underprivileged children get six weeks away from the streets or homeless shelters at a camp in North Carolina. She is also the Executive Director of Daddy's House Social Programs Incorporated, a non-profit organization that emphasizes the importance of both academics and our culture[18]. Souljah has also served as a volunteer at a medical center in Zimbabwe. There are a handful of other female rappers who continue to challenge the slave mentality by promoting charity, self-respect, and independence. But they will have to raise their voices quite a bit louder if they are to be heard above the clamor of the she-slaves. Mainstream rap is of no use to the average Black woman today. The post-Pride identity is too narrow, too simple, and too lacking in dignity to capture the essence of the Black woman. They are educators, inventors, doctors, entertainers, clergy members, athletes and mothers. From Billie Holiday to Ciara, our sisters have already proven that they can have the world hanging onto their every

---

17   *Businesses Owned by Women of Color in the United States.* Center for Women's Business Research, November 2004..

18   Daddy's House is financed by Sean "P. Diddy" Combs.

word. We are waiting for the Afrikan woman to take off her mask. We are listening for what she has to say. Before she can speak with authority, she must have knowledge of herself, her culture and her history. As it stands, the Post-pride woman's identity is built on quicksand.

CHAPTER THREE

Plastic Rap Suffocates Black Men

"The truth is that there is nothing noble in being superior to others. The only real nobility is in being superior to your former self"

—Whitney Young

We have examined some of the ways that the Willie Lynch Syndrome underlies the behavior and mentality of the Post-pride sister. These disturbing facts pale in comparison with the ravages that modern slavery inflicts on the Afrikan man's sense of self. Modern slavery is an incredible roadblock to the Afrikan man's spiritual development. It limits his aspirations. It taints his notion of peace and inhibits his regard for human life. This lowly self-image also dictates the tenor of everything that he sees, feels, and hears. All is filtered through a rigid mesh of ignorance, greed, and childish fantasy. The slave mentality dictates his total experience of life. This is the aim of all of the various degrading and violent tactics that racists use against our people. These tactics are by no means ancient history. Obama's victory over John McCain is certainly evidence that the racial climate in America has changed. But while Sambos waved signs that read "WE HAVE OVERCOME" at President Obama's inauguration, Caucasian UN aid workers pressured little Black girls in Liberia into having sex with them in exchange for the food they were supposed to be distributing for free. Teenage boys from the Congo that were working in the lava beds of Goma were being threatened with the loss of their meager wages if they did not allow UN workers from France to sodomize them. ABC News uncovered thousands of pornographic photos on United Nations Official Didier Bourgueat's (also from France) computer depicting him sexually abusing hundreds of young Congolese girls. Just weeks before the inauguration, transit cop Johannes Mehserle ruthlessly murdered a Black man who was handcuffed and lying face down on the pavement in Oakland, California. Though these details are disturbing, it is further distressing to note that millions of Post-pride brothers dance to music with lyrics that describe even greater atrocities. While most people would quickly change the radio station or go the next track on the CD, modern male slaves are thrilled by the gory accounts spewing from the speakers. They do not connect the chilling details in the songs to actual human beings with families, dreams, and rights of their own. It is enough for them that the victim was a "nigga". That's what amuses them most. *Ha ha ha. Daaaaamn! Shot that nigga!*

The aim of the Willie Lynch program is total mind control. The immensely harmful mindset of the oppressor gradually becomes the perspective of the oppressed. The Post-pride brother is extremely negative about himself and his prospects for the future, or he is childish and unrealistic about his lofty goals. In either case, he is off balance. He is surrounded by "I can't", "We'll never", "I don't have" and other false and limiting principles. All his choices are made based on these negative assumptions. He constantly blames others for his pitiful situation. In truth, the problem is a blind refusal to change. His vast potential is wasted. How many intelligent and talented brothers must we lose to this mindset? The state in which we find ourselves as a people is completely unnecessary.

It does not have to be this way. We have a tool to help us deal with moments of anger, self-doubt, sadness, and even great joy. We have our music. Afrikan music has never been about granting the wishes of those who want to destroy us. Today's so-called R&B and rap "music" is a minstrel show designed to please people who despise us. The Black pioneers of Blues, Jazz, Rock 'n Roll and R&B didn't care whether "the industry" liked their music or not. The same is true of the founders of rap music. No one was combing the streets in 1980 looking for talented rap artists. No one offered the Old School veterans a multi-million dollar contract. Our musical pioneers focused on one task- perfecting their craft. They practiced and practiced in order to develop their artistic expression, not for the guffaws and cheers of people who hated their guts. Freedom from the opinions of others is what gave them the confidence to *really get funky*. People couldn't help but gravitate towards it because the music healed them. The world often shows us its severe side. We lose loved ones, feel the effects of poverty, suffer illnesses, lose our jobs, or are the victims of crime. It is in these cloudy moments that we find the strength of our faith tested. It is at these times that we have a choice because we are standing at the meeting-place of two separate roads. We can go down one road and stew in anger, sadness, or bitterness. We can go down the other road and harvest whatever wisdom we may from the experience. Our ancestors understood very well that what was needed in those moments is a bridge to stand on as we cross over to the road to wisdom. That is the reason that Afrikan men banged furiously on their drums. This is why the Black woman stresses her voice with runs and trills. This is why the rapper speeds up his delivery, becomes almost sing-song in his rhyme, and raises the pitch of his voice. Our cultural connection to Afrika brought all of these wonderful tools to the West.

Unfortunately, modern slave music only reinforces the Black man's negative assumptions about life. He is unable to benefit from the natural and ancient healing powers of Black music. To understand the foolishness of his condition, one need only imagine a man whose city is being assaulted by a powerful hurricane. He knows that there is a shelter within walking distance. When he arrives at the shelter, the door is locked. Inside, there is warmth, food, and instructions on how to survive the storm. The man has the key to the shelter in one hand and a spatula in the other. He desperately tries, over and over, to open the lock with the spatula, ignoring the key in his other hand. After half an hour, he begins to kick in the door. It doesn't open, but it has a dent. Finally, he picks up huge rocks and starts to break all the windows. He eventually gets in, but he has destroyed his shelter. The flood waters will come seeping in through all the broken windows. He will surely drown. Afrikan music is such a shelter. Knowledge of our culture is the key. Modern slave rappers enjoy the joys of the shelter- fame and fortune- but they have bashed in and destroyed the treasures inside. Brothers are now drowning by the thousands.

Modern Music Puts Chains on the Black Man

The natural Black man sings and raps about what he loves. He is neither afraid nor is he ashamed to proclaim this to the world. Love of Black women was a consistent theme in Old School hip hop. Rakim's *I'll Be There* dealt with issues of commitment, staying together through difficult times, and raising a family. Whodini's *Friends* and *One Love* were full of intelligent observations on the challenges of relationships. They were, of course, able to make these observations without calling our people niggas and bitches. Brothers use rap to express love for our heritage as well. Doug E. Fresh's 1988 track *Africa Goin' Back Home* describes his eye-opening trip to the Mother Continent. His lyrics dispel misconceptions about Afrikan culture and he correctly points out the "brainwashing" that we have undergone in the West. Blackwatch was by far the largest Traditionalist rap clique. Its members were Brother J (Jason Hunter), the Rhythm Provider (Anthony Hardin), Grand Architect, Isis (also known as Lin Que), Queen Mother Rage, and a host of other associates. Professor X, whose given name was Lumumba Carson, was the son of prominent activist Sonny Carson. Though not picked up by the mainstream, we must not underestimate their influence upon the underground conscious rap movement. Nor can we ignore the impression they made on independent scholars in the inner cities and suburbs. Their lyrics make us excited about our history and encourage us to learn more. They were often referred to as "militant". This term is used for any person of color who speaks to the needs of their people instead of crawling around on their knees for the amusement of Caucasians. Love of self and kind is a theme picked up by a number of popular rappers. The Unbound Project is a CD put together by several rappers, including Chuck D, Talib Kweli, and The Poor Righteous Teachers. Their brave cut entitled *Mumia 911* decries the death penalty and condemns the pending execution of Mumia al Jamal. In *Mind over Matter*, Zion I implores Black men to become more mature and take care of our children. A Tribe Called Quest applies the West Afrikan method of containment to the East-West rap beef in *Keep It Moving*. We are warned to watch out for the pitfalls that were built into the system especially for us by Chuck D in Public Enemy's *First the Sheep Next the Shepherd*. And Grandmaster Flash reminds us of the manipulative nature of politicians in his 1987 track, *All Wrapped Up*.

Authentic rap music is rooted in the Afrikan's desire for community, spirituality, freedom, and dignity. This does not mean that authentic rap is only for Black people to enjoy. There are several universal themes in rap music. It is not necessary to be Black or even speak English to be a rap fan. But rap's ability to transcend culture should not be misconstrued. It does not mean that rap music "belongs" to everyone. In the same way, a Japanese person can eat enchiladas in the middle of Iceland but they are still eating *Mexican* food. Rap is rooted in Afrikan culture. The foolishness of mainstream rap cannot erase its history. Nor can it obliterate its original purpose. This begs an important question. If rap lyrics were once so full of Afrikan imagery and positive messages, how do we explain the desperate state of today's mainstream music?

D.W. Griffith's film *Birth of a Nation* debuted in 1915. It is considered an American classic. The movie attempts to show what would happen if Black men were given the right to vote, participate in government, and live in the same neighborhoods or towns as Caucasian people. There are scenes of "Negroes" picking their toes and throwing chewed-up chicken bones into the aisle during conferences on Capital Hill. "Black" men are also portrayed as rabid sexual predators that take every opportunity to attack white women. The KKK, who are the heroes of the film, eventually ride to the rescue, saving the poor, innocent white women from the depraved "Black" monsters. The "Negroes" and "Blacks" in the film were played by white actors in blackface. Very few Black people were given the opportunity to work on camera at that time. Even if we had been invited to play these roles, we probably would have declined. Black people would not intentionally portray ourselves as violent, sexual beasts. We would not knowingly humiliate ourselves on camera, behaving as though we only recently learned to walk upright. Or would we?

Compared to gangsta rap, *Birth of a Nation* is a love letter to the Black race. For the purposes of our present discussion, the term "gangsta rap" will refer to any rap music that references gangs, thug life, drug peddling, or which glorifies ignorance and Black-on-Black violence. There has always been a gangsta element in rap music. However, the early focus was on rhyming, mixing, and dancing. Gangsta rap was a localized phenomenon, concentrated in a few cities in the United States and the Caribbean. Old School rap culture had been given a chilly reception by the mainstream. Other races mocked our manner of speaking, the fat laces in our shoes, and our penchant for carrying large radios on our shoulders. Above all, the sound of rap was deemed offensive. How many times did we hear, "I can't *stand* that rap music? Those Black guys are always blasting their *boom boom boom* and I can't understand a word they're saying!" or other such remarks? But in 1987, gangsta rap became an official presence on the music scene. A clique from southern California who called themselves "Niggaz with Attitude" (NWA) released the first widely popular gangsta rap album. There were other gangsta rappers before 1987. But the coons of NWA received the most publicity. Their lyrics were brimming with genocidal threats. Suddenly, the mainstream began to love rap music. MTV launched *Yo! MTV Raps* that very same year. What was once threatening and unfamiliar became an American institution. Caucasians found that we weren't so different after all. Calling Black men "niggas" and Black women prostitutes and bitches has been a tradition in the West since we arrived. Gangsta rap exposed a cultural cross section-the disgraceful intersection between racism and volunteer slavery. It demeans us all, Afrikans and Caucasians. The brother who submerges himself in this abyss of destruction takes on the characteristics of these monsters.

The imagery in gangsta rap lyrics and videos send a clear message to the world: Black people are subhuman. We are devoid of feelings, incapable of bonding. Every Black person we meet is a potential victim. Rappers find the wailing and screaming of Black women who just lost their children hilarious as well. How many songs do we dance to have lyrics that threaten to "have ya Mama hollerin" or "make ya Moms shout"? The slave mentality is rooted in the denial of Black humanity. After all, it's only niggas! Who cares about some Black bitch's tears? Why shouldn't we dance when we hear a rapper talking about killing some worthless nigga? If there is one thing that niggas hate more than anything in the world, it's Black people. Niggas sell dope to their own kind. They abandon their children and make songs about it, supplying the world with images that liken our men to dogs, cockroaches, or other non-human males that do not rear their young. Post-pride rappers teach the world that Afrikan men couldn't care less about our sisters. Though a good portion of these rappers were themselves raised by single mothers, they joyfully recount stories of slapping, punching and kicking Black women, and even cutting their throats. The post-Pride generation despises Black women and makes every effort to degrade them in front of the whole world. Slave rap casts our sisters, who have defended, supported, and nurtured us since we stepped off of the slave ships as our enemies. Our women, who ground up glass and fed it to the slave owners who beat us, who risked their lives ferreting us away on the Underground Railroad, are bitches and hoes according to these half-dead puppets. Bitches and hoes are just as much a creation of sorry Black men as "niggas" are of racist ideology. Like the works of Cloete and E. Wallis Budge, gangsta lyrics liken our people to animals. Rappers carefully describe every detail of our anatomy and the sexual behavior of our women so that the world may know that like animals, we have no concept of intimacy.

Weak Men: The Post-Pride Generation's Gift to the Afrikan Race

In 1931, the University Of Maryland School Of Law was one of the most prestigious institutions in the country. A young Afrikan man had recently graduated from Lincoln University in Pennsylvania and decided to return to Maryland to attend law school in his home town. Though he was exceptionally bright and capable of keeping up with the work, his application was denied. The Dean informed the young man that admitting him to the school was a violation of segregation laws. That was in 1931. The culture of Black people at the time placed top priority on attending universities and opening businesses. The young man refused to give up his dreams. He applied to historically Black Howard University and was accepted. This is Afrikan culture. If we find one door closed, we instantly set about seeking one that will open. In today's R&B and rap culture, however, our story about our famous and intelligent young brother would proceed quite differently. We doubt there would even be a story because there is nothing in Post-Pride culture that encourages hard work or education in the first place. The young man's main objective would be finding unconscious sisters with no self-respect for sexual encounters and for use as personal ATM machines. His second objective would involve finding a way to dress in ridiculously expensive designer clothing. He then would look for ways to accentuate his look with gold teeth, watches, or effeminate diamond earrings. And any *nigga* who stood in his way- an elderly man who refused to hand over his wallet in a parking lot, for example- would be a *dead nigga*. (Or course, when the white police arrived, he would fall to his knees with his hands above his head and obey every order that Massa gave.) He would then write idiotic rap songs about how he had no choice but to follow a life of crime. We would hear all about how he "had to eat" and how "none of these employers was fucking with him". Post-pride culture is acidic to the Black man and therefore a direct threat against the Afrikan race. The young brother from 1931 is an example of true Afrikan manhood. Not once did he consider turning his rage against his own downtrodden people. As soon as he became a lawyer, he sued the University of Maryland and worked to overturn segregation laws. We celebrate his triumphs and ingenuity to this day. He was Thurgood Marshall, the first Afrikan American Supreme Court Justice. The most sickening aspect of Post-pride culture's effects on the Afrikan man is the weakness it injects into his psyche. Self-hate filled rap and R&B songs written by child molesters and murderers deliver the Willie Lynch message more efficiently than any slave owner ever could. These so-called 'artists' are nothing but caricatures. None of them is a real man or even a whole man.

Today's rap music is anti-intellectual. One needs neither knowledge nor education to create or enjoy it. Most of the lyrics involve selling drugs, murdering other Black people (or threatening to), and details of sexual encounters. This is not of our original culture. If it were, none of the societies on Earth would exist, for it was none other than our ancient Afrikan ancestors that spread humanity to every part of the globe. They traveled in small groups. If they had done nothing but kill each other, sell drugs, and create a bunch of fatherless children, they never would have made it. But the Sambos in the rap world thrive on internalized racism. Instead of presenting as strong, intelligent, and capable Afrikan men, they do everything that is within their power to show the world that *that is how niggas are.* Rappers mock hard-working brothers and brag about how hatred of kind has served them well. They dangle jewel-encrusted watches out of the windows of luxury automobiles. They grin like gold-toothed imbeciles as they think of amusing ways to describe how they murdered other niggas to get where they are. One does not need a brain to be part of the Post-Pride set. Their thinking centers on fighting, stealing, and pillaging. Their reasoning skills tend towards deceit and barbarism, just like the cave people. The cave people were ignorant, violent, and destructive by nature. They created no just societies nor did they practice agriculture. They didn't even practice personal hygiene and often slept atop piles of flea-infested dogs and other domestic animals. Their caves were strewn with feces and other biological waste. They lived to do three things only: eat, mate, and kill.

The Post-Pride generation's attitude towards education (as expressed via R&B and rap lyrics) has a more powerful effect on Black men than actual shackles. Since they are too lazy and unwilling to get an education, they must rely on the opinions and "ideas" of their equally lost peers. Modern slaves are the most easily manipulated generation of Black people ever to have existed. We can see quite clearly the face of Willie Lynch in all of this. Their lyrics describe school as "bullshit". They ramble on and on about how much money they are able to make without ever having to crack a book. The Post-Pride set picks up this theme. They chose that lifestyle. They disrupt our classrooms to make sure that no other Black child has an opportunity to learn, or they simply drop out of school. If they come across another Afrikan person reading or studying, they are quick to point out that *they* "ain't about to do all that damn reading". They openly discourage the Afrikan from learning altogether, citing the long years of study and the sacrifices one must make in order to graduate. Yet when their white public defenders meet them in the holding cells at the county jail, they have nothing but admiration! They never tell the educated white judge on the bench that he or she "wasted their time on that bullshit". They do not point out to the judge how they can make much more money from dealing dope. No, this attitude is reserved solely for their own people. They want to keep us all down. Massa is gone but they are going to maintain his world order in his stead. It is okay for Asian or white people to get education. But niggas only belong in the ghetto, the club, or the morgue. Today's slave rappers aim to keep us "in our place".

Rap depicts Black men as being the weakest men on the planet. Where were these legions of "niggas" when Florida decided not to count the Black votes in the 2000 election? Where were these so-called men when police in St. Petersburg, Florida chained up a 5-year old Afrikan girl and paraded her around like a slave on an auctioning block for "misbehaving in class?" What did these *niggas* who claim to have so much money and power do while Black people were dying of dehydration after Hurricane Katrina? When our own brothers and sisters were being forced to sleep next to decaying corpses in the Superdome? Of course they were nowhere to be found. The same rappers that threaten to strangle Black women in their lyrics tremble before white judges and say, "Yes Ma'am" to every order that she gives. They talk tough, but they are useless to our people. They are too busy proving that they are no threat to Massa by murdering and robbing their own kind.

Quick, Somebody Think for Me!

The modern slave mind is a small, violent world of its own. With education and diplomacy completely off the table, today's Sambos are free to move in only one direction-down. Their minds are polluted with internalized racism. Discouraging these wretched souls from perpetuating slave foolishness is nearly impossible. Human beings are incredibly resilient and can become accustomed to any circumstances. A man raised in a narrow crawlspace wouldn't know how to stand on his feet. The modern slave lives in just such a place. His world is topsy-turvy. He crawls instead of walking. When Afrikan people refer to a gangsta rapper as a "genius", what we are actually complementing is his particular style of crawling on all fours. He can string together threats and insults directed at the Afrikan race with fluidity and grace. Listen to his words. These are the dreams of every modern slave. He lives in utter darkness. He becomes even more violent when the light of truth creeps in through the heavily shuttered windows of his narrow mind. His priorities are completely out of order. A generation of Black men has been emasculated by the messages of inferiority spewing from the mouths of their beloved thug rappers. Going to the library is out of the question. Enrolling in a carpentry course is not an option. We see these types of slaves every day. They stand in groups on the street corners. They huddle on porches, blasting offensive music and spitting on the ground like cave people. Before leaving the house each day, they make sure that their pants are sagging. *I'm hopeless*, their look says. Is there anything about a man with a shower cap on his head and his pants around his ankles that says *I'm intelligent. I'm strong. I'm ready to work (or learn) right now?* Do-rags look like Jiffy Pop! Natural Black men are sickened by these slaves. It does not matter that sagging started in American prisons. Whether it came from Susanville or the moon, the fact is that of all the ways in which Black men could express themselves, they choose this unprofessional and effeminate look. These types of men then have the gall to be surprised when they are turned away from places of business. What about that look says "business" in the first place? Sagging jeans are a sign of sexual availability in American prisons. Male inmates let their underwear show to let other prisoners know that their anus is available. Some slaves are sure to argue that it originated with the fact that inmates are not permitted to wear belts. They will say that because they might be used as weapons or instruments of escape, all prisoners go beltless. In any case, sagging jeans are a sign of hopelessness. The fact that millions of Afrikan mothers and fathers encourage this behavior by dressing their children like sex-starved criminals only further nauseates us.

Groupthink reigns supreme in the minds of modern slave men. Their thoughts are a jumble of impulses. *Get some money. Kill them niggas. Fuck them hoes.* It is more difficult to escape from modern slavery than the kind experienced by our ancestors. Our forebears were able to escape because they realized that the world was big and the plantation was very small. Today's Sambos, however, have taken it upon themselves to make the world conform to the Willie Lynch Order. It therefore does not matter where they go. They will never be able to outrun their own slave minds. No white person need call them niggas because they are going to identify that way on their own. No klansman need lynch a Black person because the slaves will commit home invasions and murder us themselves. No university need deny us admission because they are not going to apply in the first place. The slave's insecurity and guilty conscience instill in him a need to be surrounded at all times by other Sambos. He is incapable of original thought and desperately stuffs his mind with the words of others. High on narcotics and alcohol, he considers himself a deep thinker. In his intoxicated state, he believes that the rapists and murderers on the mic are actually conveying some sort of metaphysical message that few can understand. He studies the lyrics. They become the blueprint for his criminality. His mind is numb. The elixir for this tragedy is education. But first task of the student is to learn how to teach himself. A slave's mind operates within the realm assigned to it by the pattern of brainwashing that we refer to as the Willie Lynch Program. Thinking on one's own and improving one's life is not a slave's business! If there is something he needs to know, Massa will tell him. He is not about to go poking around on his own in white folks' books. It is for this reason that we see so many young Afrikan men struggling in high school. They expect to be spoon-fed knowledge. They do not put forth any effort to figure coursework out on their own. Faced with a difficult assignment, many race to the Internet and submit work that has been copied and pasted. Unless it involves injuring or otherwise demeaning his own race, he cannot think for himself.

Without education, there will never be any progress in our community. If we produce no Black judges, we will always be at the mercy of white ones. If there are no Afrikans in medical research, the various illnesses that are most common to our people will go unaddressed. The one-dimensional persona promoted by the Post-pride contingent does not aspire to and is incapable of producing these types of thinkers. The Post-Pride answer to poverty is stripping, selling dope, and killing Black people. They do not enrich the community. In fact, they are responsible for more than 90% of the Black murder victims in the United States each year. Most cannot even put a roof over their own heads and are living with their mothers or other female relatives. They have no political power and no connections. Their money is quickly spent on expensive toys so they have none to contribute to any worthy Afrikan cause. This is not of our original culture. On the day that Mother Harriet and young Nalle were dragged to the courthouse, a towering, muscular Afrikan slave fought his way to the front. He swung at the judge with both fists, giving him the classic one-two knockout punch. The judge was not able to identify his assailant because he was unconscious before he hit the floor. When the education system locked us out, Thurgood Marshall banged at the doors until we were allowed to enter. When racism rears its ugly head and hard times come knocking at the Black community's door, what can a Sambo do besides gather up his sagging jeans and run away?

Keeping It Real

Modern slaves vigorously defend the genocidal, self-defeating speech in rap music. They absolve the rapper from all responsibility. He is not preaching hatred of self and kind. No, he is a street poet. He is merely describing the environment in which millions of Americans live. Violence, gangs, and narcotics surround him on all sides. When he raps, he is only telling the world how these circumstances forced him to live.

He is just keeping it real. Were there anything positive in his environment, he would rap about that. According to the Post-pride set, denying the reality of these lyrics means turning a blind eye to the desperation of inner city youth. We are unimpressed with the "street poet" argument. The assertion that the violence and decadence in rap lyrics are merely the rapper's observations is patently false. It is the slave rapper's own bloody, Willie Lynch-stained imagination that moves him to tell the world that his own people are worthless niggas. He delights in telling stories about Black people living in torment. It is, after all, where he believes we deserve to be. These slaves could just as easily tell stories about how Black women in the ghetto that barely have enough money to cover their own living expenses still find it in their hearts to buy groceries for their hungry neighbors. These rappers could tell the world about Black churches that open their doors to hungry and homeless people with donations given by their Black members. If they truly meant to "keep it real", they would let the world know that in 2008, Afrikan students in the South accounted for 21% of college students. This is amazing when we consider the fact that the percentage of Afrikans in the general population of states such as Kentucky, Delaware, and Arkansas is only 19%. If they were keeping it real, they would talk about how Ora Lee Brown of Oakland, California sent more than 15 young Afrikan sisters to college with money from her own pocket. These rappers dare to call themselves artists, but they have yet to tap into the beauty and strength that holds millions of Black families (and indeed, entire neighborhoods) together all over the world. This is what makes the Afrikan story so moving. This is what infuses our music with a quality we can only describe as *soul*. We do not simply overcome adversity. We do it with heart. We do it with grace and style. Because of his warped and infantile mind, the slave's definition of reality deviates from the standard. He has convinced himself (or allowed others to convince him) that only ugly things happen to Black people. Ugly is "real". Being murdered is real. Selling dope is real. Calling his people hoes and motherfuckers is real. Working towards a promotion on one's job is bullshit. Getting an education is bullshit. Earning money as opposed to begging or stealing is bullshit. "Keeping it real" is nothing but a way to twist Black minds into believing that it is cute to celebrate self-imposed defeat.

Today's slaves worship the spineless slave traders in the music industry because they view them as modern-day Cinderellas. For them, rappers represent the "rags-to-riches" dream that most Americans cherish. Slaves are like children. The idea that one can become extremely wealthy while doing very little work appeals to their laziness and impatience. It is also evidence of their ignorance. Rap is a business just like any other industry. The entertainers must work very hard in order to become successful. The corrupted egos of volunteer slaves are buttressed by a sense of entitlement. The world *owes* them success and wealth. This may sound strange when we consider the fact that the Willie Lynch Program calls for Black people to believe that we do not deserve anything. Today's slaves have swallowed this Program wholesale. How is it, then, that they all believe that they should be millionaires?

The answer to this question is easily understood when we examine the Sambo's sense of himself. He is a nobody, a broke ass nigga. Anyone who is not buying him clothes, drugs, vehicles, or jewelry is also a broke ass nigga. He will never be the boss because in his mind, the boss must be Caucasian. When he manages to assume some measure of power or attain financial freedom, he believes that he has come as close as possible to being white. He has Massa's clothes, shoes, cars, and toys. He cannot put on Massa's face (Michael Jackson's grotesque transformation notwithstanding), but he can wear Massa's attitude. He believes that being rich (thus, exercising Massa's prerogative) is the solution to his problems. The truth is that he becomes more obnoxious and dangerous to Black people as a result of his newfound status. He is "playing white"- standing in the slave Massa's shoes. He works hard to prove his loyalty to his imaginary Massa by keeping his foot on the necks of other Black people to ensure that they stay in their place. His greatest fear is having another Afrikan compete with him for Massa's affection. This is why working with Sambos is so dangerous. He wants to shine in Massa's eyes all by himself. When Sambos are in power, they are more brutal towards Black people than any other race. We are aware that one of the police officers that murdered Sean Bell in New York is Black. Black cops and correctional officers are particularly vicious against Afrikan inmates and suspects. A similar situation existed in South Afrika. The natives should have been able to expect some measure of decency and understanding from their own kind. But as soon as the bloodthirsty Europeans handed them badges and guns, they attacked other natives with unbelievable rapacity. We find this in dozens of Afrikan countries today whose Presidents are nothing more than well-dressed buffoons. They are cartoonish imitations of the thieving, treacherous colonial administrations of the 1950's. This is because Sambos cannot fathom any Black person being a legitimate leader. When they have money or the power to rule, their first question is, "What would Massa do?" Hip hop appeals to hundreds of thousands of weak, slave-minded Black men because it reinforces the idea that Black people only gain influence and authority by robbing, selling dope and behaving like cave people- all at the expense of other Afrikans.

Whether we are British, Ghanaian, or American, Black people understand that we have witnessed the dawning of an era in which a new type of Afrikan man is emerging. His focus is on education, family, and progress. He is not interested in being a thug. He may struggle from time to time. He might even stumble, but he refuses to fall into the suffocating, bottomless pit that is the slave mind. He is the architect of a bright future for his family and our people. We say that this is a "new" type of Afrikan man, but he is only new to those who know nothing about our culture except what is offered by the Post-Pride set. He is actually a modern version of what the Black man has been from the time he first drew breath on this planet millions of years ago.

Black men have centuries of history and endless heroes to learn from and emulate. We employ the example of William Perry because his story is illustrative of the power of the "new" Afrikan to which we now refer. In 1888, Henry Ford purchased a large piece of land on which he planned to build a new home. He hired William Perry (originally from Canada) to help him clear the land. There were no high-powered electric saws back then. They used a saw that had handles on each end. With Ford on one end and Perry on the other, they toiled for weeks until the job was done. Years later, Perry (who was quite a bit older than Ford) retired from physical labor and was in need of a white collar job. He contacted Henry Ford. In 1914, William Perry became the first Black man to hold a position in corporate America. We fear for the younger generations when we compare Perry's attitude with that of today's Sambos.

The Sambo never would have gotten a chance to work in corporate America because he would have turned sour in 1888 after finding out that all he was going to be doing was cutting down trees. He would have made himself angry by calculating how much money Ford had and bitterly dreaming about the position that Ford "should" have given him. Perry opened doors for thousands of Afrikan Americans because of his work ethic and integrity. Two years after he started working in the corporate office, 50 more Black men were hired by the Ford Company. The Henry Ford Trade School also changed the lives of many Black families by offering training to both Black and Caucasian people. Ford also paid equal wages to both races, something that was revolutionary at the time.

The Afrikan community benefits from the accomplishments of the new Afrikan man. His ventures create employment and educational opportunities in our communities. Our families are able to enjoy a higher standard of living. We reap the spoils of stability and generational progress. We also benefit from established political connections. These connections are vital to our growth and survival. We need to get on the inside! We can sing and march until we lose our voice and our feet are sore. Unless we have support from the Senate and House floors, we are wasting our breath and our precious feet. We made the mistake of letting our guard down after the Civil Rights Movement. We turned our backs on the power of communalism and education. President Obama's victory must not be interpreted as the end of the struggle. President Obama is but one man. The Civil Rights Movement is about tens of millions of Afrikan men, women, and children. The Civil Rights Movement set a high standard of dignity and placed an enormous value on upward mobility and political strength. Far too many of us have made a conscious decision to "keep it real", to wallow in the genocidal abominations that are every slave's dream. Since 70% of the rap in this country is purchased by Caucasians, we may conclude that it is their dream as well.

The "Conscious Rapper" Myth

Certain rap and R&B entertainers distinguish themselves with the title "conscious". They claim that the substance of their music is more culturally grounded and politically relevant than that of gangsta rappers. Conscious rappers are pseudo-intellectuals who may have read the opening paragraphs to one or two books while in prison or before dropping out of college. They use music as a platform for their convoluted slave babble. Their lack of intellect is indeed laughable! These Sambos believe that they impress us by dropping quotes from Bruce Lee, famous Mafia figures, and other uneducated rappers. Unfortunately, these quotes are usually inaccurate or attributed to the wrong person. Other sources of their "knowledge" include the Bible and Quran. Both texts have been twisted and misquoted to support their own petty little slave ideas.

Many rappers seek to impart their bizarre notion of religion to their audience. These "religions" apparently promote the sale of drugs, pimping, and murdering Black people. One especially ignorant East Coast rapper suggested that gangs get together and agree not to "gangbang around the kids". We challenge this sniveling idiot to find a place in America, Jamaica, or England where there no children walking down the streets. It is impossible not to gangbang around the children because *gangs are made up of kids* who went down the wrong path. When we examine the lyrical content of "conscious rap", we find it to be no different from gangsta rap. Afrikan people are still, according to "conscious rappers", a worthless bunch of niggas and hoes that are only good for buying their dope, being sexual objects, or target practice. It is a case of the blind leading the blind. This is what happens in the absence of education. Whenever an Afrikan points this out to a modern slave, that miserable slave instantly begins to recite a few lines of lyrics from popular rap music that might make it appear that the slave entertainer actually cares about something other than himself. What a ridiculous way to prove a point! If he or she is a natural Afrikan rapper, *all* of their tracks should be filled with humor, wisdom, and respect for the Black race. One should not have to sift through lines and lines of bitches and motherfuckers just to find a few crumbs of knowledge. We can pick up any Earth, Wind & Fire CD and *all of the tracks on it praise Black humanity and celebrate Life*. We can play any James Brown track at random without once hearing that we are worthless niggas or that we deserve to be shot.

Our voluntary return to mental bondage is a source comfort to racists. Black people with the slave mentality are "in their place". It does not matter how much money they make. They are million dollar slaves wrapped in platinum chains. Racists are not threatened by our money made from selling drugs, robbing, and rapping. The only possible danger is that one of these happy slaves might break his neck while rushing to hand his money back to Massa. They make more money for Caucasians than slaves ever did. There is no way that a single slave could have chopped enough wood or cotton to purchase million-dollar homes. All Afrikan men have been tainted by this image. It did not begin with hip hop. The stigma attached to being a Black man in the West goes back nearly half a millennium. The difference is that *we* are telling the world that this is who we are. The world believes us. After all, we should know. Slaves are not going to do anything about being disrespected except kill one another and hand their money over to Caucasians. What happy and obedient slaves we've become!

The New Afrikan Man

There must be a culture that incubates the new Afrikan mind. We must be able to ground ourselves in our music and our shared values. We find evidence of the new mentality emerging among several popular entertainers. After over a decade of stagnation, R&B (and its sister genre, Neosoul) are beginning to produce quality music with lyrics indicative of the progressive era. Many of these artists are returning to the poetic lyrics of the 1980's while taking advantage of today's advanced production techniques. They manage to incorporate the new without throwing away the old. Olu's *Beautiful Place* (2005) is one example. The South can certainly be proud of entertainers such as Anthony David (*Acey Duecy*) and Kenne Wayne (*You're The Best, 2008*). Wendell B.'s *Definition of a Real Man* could easily be the anthem for the new Afrikan man. If we are to move forward as a group, we need music that reflects the issues and priorities of the progressive Afrikan man. Veteran soul singer Al Green's *Lay It Down* is a blueprint for up and coming performers. So many young brothers have powerful, beautiful voices. But these voices are wasted on lyrics that describe fornicating in clubs or other public places as if we were animals. Al Green's romantic prose sets both an example and a standard for the new generation of Black male vocalists.

Though most of the rap world is still wallowing in slave foolishness, we are able to find evidence of a new type of thinking in the lyrics of several entertainers. In 2000, Dead Prez expressed their concern for Black people's health in their release *Be Healthy*. They encourage us to take more pride in our bodies and urge us to quit smoking cigarettes. Gza's *Pro Tools* (2008) gave us an opportunity that we have been denied for years: a chance to enjoy sizzling beats without being called niggas or having our lives threatened. Jurassic 5's song *Contribution*, also released in 2000, explores relationships between Black men and women. These brothers point out our lack of gratitude towards our women and denounce domestic violence. In 1999, The Roots gave us *Act Too...The Love of My Life*. The ever-conscious Blackalicious thrilled us with *Lotus Flower* in 2005. Their use of ancient Kemetic imagery (the lotus flower) and the vocals of funk legend George Clinton was an imaginative statement of ancestral reverence. Common also took us back to the Pride Era in *The Corner*. On this track, the Last Poets revive slogans from the Civil Rights Movement, such as "Black is Beautiful" and "Black Power". They describe gatherings between brothers as "testimonials to freedom, peace, and love". We are heartened by these efforts. It signals an awakening of the Afrikan identity after such a long and miserable slumber. Self-preservation is also slowly returning to rap music, with M-1 (of Dead Prez) railing against the slave lunacy that is rotting our community from within (*Confidential*, 2006). The Coup's *Fuck a Perm* urges us not to allow Europeans to dictate our definition of beauty. It also ridicules the self-hatred that prompts unconscious Black men to mock women with natural Afrikan hair. In recent years, we have also seen a revival of Afrikan-centered terminology. This language, often described as "cultic" speaks directly to the in-group without being exclusionary. The song is for everyone to enjoy, but the message speaks specifically to Afrikan people. This is different from today's slave lingo, which seeks to unite people of all colors under a banner of Black degradation. In *Big Dreams*, Bow Wow tells our young people to work hard and never give up on their goals. He warns against trying to take shortcuts to the top. The lyrics of *Big Dreams* expose selling drugs and hanging with the thugs as poor choices that put us in our graves. The lyrics are very personal. They are speaking directly to us. DJ Jazzy Jeff's *Return of the Magnificent* (2008) is loaded with lyrics suggesting Black unity and personal responsibility. Tracks like *Run That Back* and *Come On* are prime examples of new Afrikan thinking. Unlike the slave rappers who seek to give every bit of our culture to anyone who will sit still long enough, The Perceptionists use their track *Black Dialogue* to claim our heritage. They remind the imitators that this is Afrikan culture and that it belongs to the Afrikans. We are awakening. The Afrikan falcon is testing his wings. He is learning just how boundless and pristine the heavens can be when one is warmed and fueled by his inner Afrikan sun.

The Afrikan Notion of Celebrity

Although it would be refreshing to see the hip hop world leading the younger generations towards the light, we do not know that this positive momentum will continue to build. Black men must move on whether the rap world redeems itself or not. The cure for what ails us is can be found in a return to our roots. One would imagine that our Afrikan ancestors worshipped their popular singers. After all, music is a central aspect of West Afrikan cultures. Our research has determined that this was not the case. Our people considered their singers to be ordinary people who were doing a job. If they performed well, they were paid well and invited to entertain again. They were not given the high regard that cattle and sheep herders (for example) enjoyed. The reason for this is obvious. Cattle and sheep herders fed the nation and kept the economy going. Singers merely provided candy for our ears. They are entertainers, not gods. They are dancers and singers. They are not life-saving surgeons. They are not teachers going into the trenches every day and struggling to give us the next generation of doctors, attorneys, and architects. In our culture, it is what a man does- not what he has- that distinguishes him and places him among the Great Ones. The progressive Afrikan man cannot be misled by the gold-toothed slave catchers in the entertainment business. He sees past their shiny toys and scantily-clad strumpets. He sees through their empty words and bloody threats, straight into their empty and enslaved souls.

CHAPTER FOUR

Big Shackles for Little Afrikans

"Therefore, if you break the female, she will break the offspring in its early years of development and, when the offspring is old enough to work, she will deliver it up to you... Train the female horse whereby she will eat out of your hand, and she will train the infant horse to eat of your hand also." -From "Let's Make A Slave" By Willie Lynch as published by The Black Arcade Liberation Library; 1970.

"Our children will not survive our habits of thinking, our failures of the spirit, our wreck of the universe into which we bring new life so blithely. Mostly, our children will resemble our own misery and spite and anger, because we give them no choice about it."

—June Jordan

Essential Ingredients of a Healthy Afrikan Mind

A letter from President Barack Obama to his daughters Natasha (Sasha) and Malia was posted in Parade Magazine in January of 2009. We include a portion of the letter here in order to acquaint the reader with its substance:

Dear Malia and Sasha,

I know that you've both had a lot of fun these last two years on the campaign trail, going to picnics and parades and state fairs, eating all sorts of junk food your mother and I probably shouldn't have let you have. But I also know that it hasn't always been easy for you and Mom, and that as excited as you both are about that new puppy, it doesn't make up for all the time we've been apart. I know how much I've missed these past two years, and today I want to tell you a little more about why I decided to take our family on this journey.

When I was a young man, I thought life was all about me—about how I'd make my way in the world, become successful, and get the things I want. But then the two of you came into my world with all your curiosity and mischief and those smiles that never fail to fill my heart and light up my day. And suddenly, all my big plans for myself didn't seem so important anymore. I soon found that the greatest joy in my life was the joy I saw in yours. And I realized that my own life wouldn't count for much unless I was able to ensure that you had every opportunity for happiness and fulfillment in yours. In the end, girls, that's why I ran for President: because of what I want for you and for every child in this nation.

Afrikan Americans swelled with pride as we read the letter. Obama's unabashed tenderness towards his children is symbolic of one of the most joyous aspects of Black culture. Afrikans love children. Western education and structural modernization have not dimmed the Afrikan woman's fervent wish to experience motherhood. West Afrikans express their notion of the sacredness of childhood in many colorful ways. Until fairly recently, the Bubi woman became exempt from any form of physical labor from the time she gave birth until the child was walking. Her husband was even forbidden from asking her to do something as simple as handing him a glass of water.

The Bubi belief that childhood is a holy time even extends to the woman that brought him into the world. The Bangloan people celebrate the birth of children with feasts and visits from the local priests. The birth of twins is a particularly festive event for the Bangloan. They consider twins to be special children of God. At the end of their lives, twins are buried in the same elaborate fashion as the Bangloan King. Our adoration of children in modern times has not waned, but the ways in which this celebration manifests itself has changed. Black churches in the United States save space in their weekly bulletins for the accomplishments of children in the congregation. High SAT scores, good grades, college acceptance letters, and several other achievements are read aloud so that the entire church family can be proud. In South Afrika, National Children's Day is commemorated each year with a forum on youth welfare that is attended by educators and government officials.

Children are essential to every society. Their presence makes possible the continuation of the community. They are also future guardians of the culture. It is therefore crucial that the children be healthy. They must be mentally stable, emotionally resilient, and physically sound. They must one day be able to not only maintain the current conditions in a society, but also improve upon them. A stagnant society suffers. Lack of medical advances, inadequate defense technology, and a quickly changing and violent world make a potent recipe for extinction. Nations that fail to make ideological advances also suffer from a dirth of fresh ideas and new, modern ways of expressing spirituality. Children are the personification of any community's potential. Future generations may make incredible contributions to our quality of life.

A child is a blank canvas. His or her experiences are like brushstrokes on that canvas. The totality of these experiences-plus the child's ability to make positive conclusions from whatever befalls him- determine his or her picture of life. The family (and the community which is an extension of the family) is charged with the task of helping the child make sense of the squiggles and lines of life's encounters. This is a weighty obligation. The child must enter into adulthood believing that the universe is a friendly and helpful place. He must also believe he is an extension of this grand universe; a vital player in the universal drama of infinite hospitality and Goodness. Spacious homes, designer clothing, video games and mp3 players all offer some measure of comfort and happiness to those that can afford them. But they do not prepare the child to make sense of his world. Successful child-rearing in all its many forms appears to be more closely related to the parent's wisdom of the priceless, invisible aspects of life. In other words, the unseen possessions of the heart- love, forgiveness, gratitude, humble determination- absolutely must be passed from parent to child. Shiny toys and $500 gaming systems are optional. We do not mean to imply that a person may not acquire the aforementioned finer qualities as an adult. There are a number of examples of famous Black people who have overcome desperate and cruel childhood experiences. These Afrikans managed to aspire to something higher than the ideas and behaviors they had known as children.

Safety is naturally a priority in every society because of a child's naivite and innocence. Children understand very little about the world. It does not matter how perfect their grades are or how high their SAT scores. He or she is lacking in wisdom and in dire need of guidance. Afrikan children's needs differ from those of other races because of their unique history and precarious social circumstances. Afrikan children in England, Jamaica, Brazil, and America are victims of an institutionalized and racially-based legacy of poverty and debt. In addition, they must struggle against a manufactured identity that is marketed towards them by slave-catchers disguised as entertainers. Black youth must also cope with the societal disease of racism. It affects our children on several different levels. It can mean attending underfunded schools and substandard health care. It can even mean being savagely beaten or murdered by the police. Furthermore, the sheer violence of the modern age threatens the well-being of our children. We are all familiar with reports of school shootings, kidnappers lurking on the Internet, and a host of other terrors.

Our children cannot flourish in the absence of stability. Constant upheavals in the family or many tragedies in their neighborhood threaten the child's understanding of the world as a loving place. The violence at the heart of modern hip hop lyrics sow the seeds of disruptiveness and instablility in young Afrikan minds. We need only note the examples of war-torn places in Afrika (such as the Congo and Somalia) to understand that nothing can thrive when it is constantly being torn apart. Little Afrikans also need boundaries to reinforce their notion of stability. Boundaries assist in the maturation process. This is easy to observe in nature. When one wishes to grow tomatoes or flowers, one begins by clearing and tilling a plot of land. In so doing, one creates a boundary between the refined soil and wilderness. Each irrigation ditch is also a boundary. It marks off the small strip of soil that is allotted to each stalk. What would happen if the gardener simply threw handfuls of seeds into unmarked wilderness? Some of the seeds might grow, but most of the resources of sunlight and water would be wasted. The gardener would find himself watering places where there were no seeds and under-watering areas with lots of seeds. This is why boundaries exist. They allow parents to focus on the essential aspects of child-rearing instead of the many trifling ones. The brash, vulgar, and anti-Afrikan messages in modern rap and R&B show no evidence of boundaries. Nothing is sacred in hip hop. Black children must also be raised with an emphasis on advancement. The emphasis in hip hop culture is on sex, materialism, and genocide. Sadly, many Afrikan parents allow their children to imitate the wretched slaves on television today.

It did not take long for Black children on plantations to learn that they were slaves. There was nothing in their surroundings that recognized, let alone celebrated, their humanity. Every element of their environment was designed to reinforce the concepts of submission, indignity, and inferiority. Captives were not allowed to be children. As soon as they were toilet trained, they were carrying firewood, drawing buckets of water, and helping in the kitchen. They were taught from the moment they were born that all Black people were inferior and worthless. Lamentably, Black children are just as misinformed about their culture and identity today as they were 138 years ago. The difference is that this time, the Afrikan community is the source of that misinformation.

Black children waste an appalling amount of time watching television. According to the Child Trends Databank, school-age Afrikan children watch 4 or more hours of television per day. They are exposed to racist imagery, foul language, lewdness, blasphemy, and violence- and that's just the cartoons!

They watch music videos, buy CDs, and go to the cinema with their friends. What are they learning about our heritage when they watch these music video channels? They learn that Black men are extremely violent. They learn that Black women are the nastiest females on Earth and that we all love selling crack, taking ecstasy and crystal meth. When they watch specials entitled "NAACP Image Awards" and "Black Entertainment Television Awards", they learn to associate Blackness with the individuals who win. Modern minstrels receive trophies for preaching genocide and self-hatred and our children think that's what it means to be Black. Post-Pride "culture" attacks every part of the Afrikan identity. It teaches our children to love their enemies and murder their friends. We are able observe the effects of this kind of brainwashing in nature. Among the ants is a species called "slaver" ants. Slavers raid the nests of other ants, carrying off their larvae and pupae. The slavers then raise the kidnapped ants as their own. When they reach maturity, the enslaved ants will give their lives for their new colonies. They will even attack their own kind to defend their captors. The kidnapped ants no longer know which species they are because they identify with the slavers. Black parents allow their children to be saturated with messages of hatred of self and kind. The impressionable Afrikan child learns from an early age that our people belong on the lowest rung of the societal ladder. They learn from the minstrels on television and radio that we are to be despised, hunted, and killed. They do not see other Afrikans as extensions of themselves. They identify with the slaves on television. Is there any surprise that they grow up, tote guns, and murder their own kind?

Today's Afrikan youth suffer from cultural neglect. Black people have failed to impress upon our children the value of our heritage and traditions. We pawn this responsibility off on the Public School System. Apparently, many Black parents have the resources to buy their children expensive athletic shoes, jewelry, and violent, racist video games, but none for books and documentaries. When it comes to learning their identity, Afrikan children are left to their own devices. They are abandoned to the television set, where the media assigns them heroes that were selected by the music industry. Our children's impressionable minds are continuously bombarded with larger than life images of gangstas, thugs, and whores. Though their behavior is both slave-like and disgusting, our children still see them with cash, jewelry, beautiful women, and luxury cars. They learn that becoming a slave can be quite lucrative. In fact, the more they disrespect our heritage, the greater the reward. For in addition to material gains, rappers are given a sort of immunity for the indecencies they commit. Black men do not stand up to rappers who disrespect our women and mislead our children. The media rewards these slaves by putting their faces on television, on magazine covers, and the silver screen. As a result, millions of Afrikan children all over the world seek to emulate gangstas and hoes. That's what being Black means for them.

However disturbing it may be, our children have the distinction of being the pool from which the next generation of slaves will be taken. The 6 and 11 year-olds of today are expected to fill the work camps, county jails, and penitentiaries in the future. They are also expected to lead scores of innocent Black people down the same path. They are expected to be tomorrow's slave-catchers. The maggots in the street gangs and the Sambos in R&B need our children to perpetuate the type of cultural climate that permits and encourages volunteer slavery.

But even a child has a concept of dignity. A child knows enough to love herself and her family. She knows enough to feel insulted if someone were to call her a *bitch* or assault her. The Afrikan child must be brainwashed into believing that she (and all Afrikans by extension) deserve a lifestyle that is on par with (and in some cases, inferior to) that of wild animals. This belief is not natural to Black people. We are sheltered by the three pillars of Afrikan culture. Today's slave-catchers realize this. Their first course of action is to destroy the Afrikan child's cultural shield.

The Middle Passage

Communalism is conspicuously absent from today's hip hop culture. The message of rap is "I gotta get mine, regardless." Black people are depicted as being perpetually predatory; robbing, beating, and murdering our own kind. Post-Pride culture is divisive. Slave rappers happily encourage their audience to kill other Black people based on the neighborhoods in which we live. They praise gang banging and turf wars. Our children are told to "leave a nigga dead" if he "gets in the way". Rappers honor dope dealers by calling them *soldiers*. They actually believe that selling poison to sick people is a thing to be admired. The slave minds admires those who fragment and destroy rather than inspire and uplift our people. Gone is the ancestral reverence of the Old School era. Our inventions, accomplishments, and history mean so little that for them, a single word sums up all that we are and all that we have been. Today's slaves call themselves "niggas" and permit their Caucasian "friends" to do the same. The indiscriminate use of the words "bitch" and "hoe" are inconsistent with the matriarchal societies from which we descend. Rappers no longer praise our people and our legacy in their lyrics. If anything, they seek to obliterate our cultural treasures. How many Old School tracks have today's happy slaves ruined? How many tracks by Parliament, Debarge, and James Brown have been befouled by lyrics that promote selling dope, slapping, kicking, and choking our women? The explicit lyrics of rap run counter to another distinguishing feature of Afrikan culture. Those of us who were born prior to the post-Pride era were raised with an understanding that certain topics were "grown folks' business". We were rarely permitted to listen to "grown folks talking" and never allowed to participate. Adults provided Black children with a space that was all our own; where we were free to be children. At family and church gatherings, people quickly separated into two groups- children and grown folks. It was a product of our heritage. Being a child is just a sacred a role as being an adult. Each should be given their own sphere in which to socialize, learn, and grow. There are no boundaries in post-Pride culture. Our children are right in the middle of it all. They are learning to be better slaves every day.

This misidentification causes many Black children to tailor their speech to what is "appropriate" for niggas. Black boys as young as 5 years of age refer to themselves as "pimps". Our young girls use filthy language and call Black boys "niggas". Our babies also imitate the grammar of rap music, which is indeed unfortunate. Ebonics is a lyrical and expressive dialect, but our children are in need of sound grammatical skills. How are Black children ever going to compete, academically and professionally, if they can't even speak the official language? Why do we have money to buy our children music that teaches them how to perform oral sex but none for a set of educational

DVDs? And since the vulgar language in rap music is acceptable, our children conclude that the uncivilized behavior that it describes is acceptable as well. It becomes normal to participate in brawls and carry weapons. Their young minds memorize the various models and calibers of assault weapons listed in rap songs. Many know how to use guns before they have actually handled one. Black children are also introduced to drugs at extremely early ages via post-Pride rap lyrics. Little Black boys know the terminology for heroin, cocaine, and ecstasy. They learn the going price for grams and ounces of dope. It is not a big leap for them to then begin selling and/or using drugs on their own.

Black children also rush out in droves to experiment with the unbridled sexuality of post-Pride rap. From the time they are able to sit still long enough, they sit in front of the television watching ¾ naked Black women flirting with the camera like prostitutes campaigning for tricks. These same women then go on to make movies and commercials that are aired during children's programs. Our young girls learn that this is the way they must behave if they want to be successful in life. The media pressures them into dressing like sluts, but Black parents are to blame. It is appalling and outrageous. Girls as young as 7 years old cavort through the neighborhood in low-riding jeans that expose their backsides and/or undergarments. Their parents buy them bare mid-drift shirts, skin-tight jeans, backless shirts and even thongs. In so doing, they invite sexual advances from males of all ages upon girls who have not even reached adolescence. Little Black girls are saturated with sexual suggestions and imagery. In imitation of their role models in the rap world, they bend over, squat, and shake their backsides like disease-ridden prostitutes. Many Black adults encourage this behavior. They find these dances "cute". Our little sisters can be seen in their front yards, on the playground at school, and even *on street corners* rolling and gyrating like strippers. They become comfortable with foul language and overt sexuality. It is then quite easy- almost natural- for them to begin having sexual relations. In 2000, 2.4 out of every 1000 Black girls in the United States between the ages of 10 and 14 became mothers. For girls aged 15–17, the rate was 50 per 1000[19]. 20% of Black women have babies before they are 20 years old[20]. Two out of ten Black women has her education interrupted because of a pregnancy. Afrikan girls do not have far to look to find sexual partners. Post-Pride culture teaches our boys that frequent, often anonymous encounters with hoes are part of being a nigga. The sacredness of sexuality is lost amid vivid descriptions of genitalia, oral and anal sex, and ejaculation. Before they reach puberty, they too are engaging in every variety of sexual behavior. The Afrikan community puts our cultural stamp of approval on these antics by allowing our children to speak, dress, and behave in the post-Pride fashion.

What else is there for today's miseducated Black youth? Because they have not been taught who we truly are, they confine their aspirations to what is appropriate for niggas and hoes. Many dream of being dope dealers, pimps, and strippers instead of doctors and engineers. Education is worthless to many Black children. They have been taught neither its value nor our historical struggle for access. They have no interest in the one thing that can help them break their psychological

---

19   J.A. Martin, B. E. Hamilton, et al. *Births: Final Data for 2000*. National Vital Statistics Report.

20   *Teenagers in the US: Sexual Activity, Contraception Use, and Childbearing: 2000*. Center for Disease Control and Prevention.

chains- an education. Parents must take responsibility for teaching our children at home. Their schoolwork must be supplemented with cultural material that fosters a healthy sense of identity. Children learn faster and with greater zeal when they are studying their own culture. Autumn Ashante of New York was a nationally recognized poet by the age of 7. She was home-schooled by her father. She recently came under fire for a poem she wrote entitled "White Nationalism Put U in Bondage". The poem was her reaction to a mural at a public school that depicted Black people kneeling at the feet of Abraham Lincoln. Lincoln is seated in the mural with his arms outstretched in a manner reminiscent of Jesus. Middle aged Caucasian men on radio talk shows and cable network news programs showered her with threats and insults. One went so far as to scream, "IF YOU WANT TO GO BACK TO AFRIKA, I WILL PERSONALLY BUY YOU A TICKET." Interviewers and commentators are constantly suggesting that Autumn's father is actually the author of her poems. They say that no 7-year old could come up with ideas such as hers. These same newscasters that condemn the content of her poems would dedicate a half-hour show to her if she put on tight clothes and rolled her hips like a stripper. They would consider her a child prodigy if only she would act like a slave.

Afrikan Children: Lost and Turned Out

The post-Pride mentality destroys Black children's self-esteem. Though fancy cars, women, and money are associated with being a nigga, very little else of value is. Therefore, in the absence of flashy material items, they feel that they are worthless. Being a nigga in a limousine is ideal, but a broke nigga is a disgrace.

Afrikan children do not usually have access to cash, jewelry, and cars at the age of 12 and 13. In their minds, they are worthless little niggas until the day that they have platinum watches, $80K automobiles and thick wads of cash. With little education and no role models, their chances of obtaining these trinkets through legal means are indeed slim. The South Afrikan branch of the Institute for Security Studies conducted a 10-nation study of children involved in organized crime in 2005. The ISS is an organization dedicated to the research, debate, and implementation of security policies relevant to Afrikan people. They found that Black children from Brazil, Jamaica, Nigeria, South Afrika and the United States become involved with gangs at very early ages- 13 ½ years on average. They are introduced to thug life by older teens in their neighborhoods and their friends at school. Sometimes older family members "help" our young people get into gangs. Black teenagers report that they become involved in gangs for status, material goods, and girls[21]. Our children sell drugs, prostitute themselves, fight, and commit murders in order to have the very trinkets for which slave rappers have sold their souls.

Black men are responsible for this insanity. Far too many Black men spend all their time worrying about having the latest shoes and earrings so that they can look "cute" and they forget all about their own babies. Sisters are left to take care of the children on their own. The Poverty in the United States: 2000 study revealed that "Black children are less likely than White or Hispanic children to live in a married-couple family. In 2000, 37 percent of Black children under the age of 18 lived

---

21   *Young Guns: Children in Organized Crime.* Published in Crime Quarterly, Number 14, 2005.

in two-parent families and 53 percent lived in single-parent families." 78 percent of White children and 65 percent of Hispanic children live in two-parent homes. Black female-headed households were 6 times more likely to live below the poverty line than Black married-couple families. 31% of Afrikan American children live below the poverty line[22]. In Mississippi and Louisiana, our people live in crumbling shacks and under conditions that mimic those of third world countries. The poverty figure of 31% is misleading. The US Department of Health and Human Services set the poverty line at $15,260 for a family of three[23]. Many of our people live off of little more than that but are not counted as "poor". In the inner cities, Black children play among discarded condoms, liquor bottles, syringes, and diapers. They jump and wrestle on urine and semen soaked mattresses. Yellow police tape has replaced the makeshift kites of the former generations. Black children can be seen running through the ghettoes with fists full of these yellow streamers. They live under cramped conditions. This leads to an underdeveloped sense of privacy. It is the reason that our children swear, fornicate, steal, and fight without even realizing that they have broken the social code.

Given the ramifications of absentee fathers, it is frightening that baby daddies are en vogue in popular culture. Post-pride culture teaches that it is "cute" when brothers have children in every corner of the city. But with each new baby mama, Black men have less time and resources to contribute to each

---

22   US Department of Commerce, Bureau of the Census: *Poverty in the United States 2000.*
23   US Department of Health and Human Services: 2003 Federal Poverty Guidelines.

child's upbringing. Of course, this only applies to brothers who actually stay in the picture. Many of our children do not have fathers at all. The 2003 figure of 69 percent out of wedlock births is a stark representation of this fact. Some might point out that being born out of wedlock does not mean that the father is absent. We must admit that this is true. The problem arises when men fail to live up to the duties of fatherhood. Unless a man can name his child's favorite book, favorite toy, cartoon, and snack, he cannot call himself a father. Unless a man consistently contributes to the child's housing, clothing, and medical expenses, he is not a father. He is a stick figure. Many Sambos claim that they cannot be a father because they did not have a father themselves. This makes absolutely no sense. Did he so enjoy the poverty and neglect that he wishes to share it with his own children? There are only two reasons for the absence of Black fathers: self-hatred and cowardice. Abandoning our children teaches them that Black people are inferior. They look around and none of their friends have fathers. *After all,* many of our children think, *if our own fathers didn't want us, we must be pretty worthless.* Even serial killers' fathers come to court for them and plead for mercy. Many innocent Black children have never even seen their fathers. They grow up seeing other children enjoying relationships with their fathers, but no one is there for them. In school, our fatherless children burn with shame when asked, "What does your father do?" Something inside of them breaks every time they are asked to draw a picture of their family and they do not even know how their father looks. While other children are making Fathers Day cards, they dream about what it would be like to have a father who cared for them. Black men sentence their children to shame, loneliness, and extreme poverty when we turn our backs on them.

For many Black children, it makes no difference whether they realize that they have broken taboos or not. They curse in public and no one cares. They refuse to give seats to elderly and handicapped people on the bus and no one cares. We are no longer proud Black people who work together to monitor the children in our neighborhoods. Gone are the days when any Black adult on our block could correct wayward children and expect to be obeyed. That was when we were *Black people,* not niggas. That was when we had pride. This is the post-Pride era. The image we waive around for all to see and enjoy is one of a people who care nothing about one another. Our babies do not feel protected or valued. The only way for them to take some measure of control over their lives is by attacking their own people. Little Black boys sell drugs to get money to control girls and other boys, poisoning Black people in the process. Our little girls use the extreme sexuality of post-Pride culture to manipulate little boys. They have sex and perform other inappropriate "favors" for these boys to get the attention that they do not get at home. Rap lyrics and videos help them along by offering unlimited tips on how to become a "bad bitch". The Black community is silent while our children's lives are being ripped apart. We continue to support this slave music. We continue to dress our children like these modern slaves. The message we send to our children is that this is who we are.

Tiny Coffins

Gangsta rap fosters a love of genocide in Black children. Thugs are their heroes. Afrikan children can often be heard repeating lyrics that give graphic details of murders, of bullets tearing through flesh and the way that corpses smell. But they do not have to listen to rap music to learn these things today. The past 5 years have been open season on Black children in the United States. The first half of 2006 alone brought these images to life for many. A Dallas mother was shot to death in front of her daughters as she was loading a moving van. Friends told the local news channel that she was leaving to escape the violence in her neighborhood. In Trenton, New Jersey, 8 year-old Tajanee Lee was shot in the face as she rode her bicycle. Rival gang members were firing on a van that was driving down the street and a "stray" bullet struck the little sister. All of the witnesses to the incident described the heart-wrenching screams of her aunt as she ran to see what had happened. 6 people had already been shot in her neighborhood that week. Also in 2006, a 19 year-old gang member shot Siretha White of Chicago to death at her 11th birthday party. Her murder was witnessed by all of the children who attended. 14 year-old Starkesia Reed (also of Chicago) was shot and killed while looking out her living room window. These are unfortunately just a few of the Black children who lost their lives to the senseless savagery that our community seems to think is so "cute" for our children to emulate. Black children know violence. They know death. Children in the predominantly Afrikan West Englewood section of Chicago have a horrific rate of hospitalizations from gunshots. An average of 98 children out of every 100,000 was shot between 1999 and 2001 alone[24]. Black children continue to love violent videos and lyrics even though it devastates their lives. They simply do not know any better. Because they have not been taught, they have little chance of comprehending -let alone navigating- a system that was designed to destroy us all more than 300 years ago.

---

24   Children's Memorial Research Center.

The New Afrikan Child

If our children are to survive the modern era, they must be reared with a new type of consciousness. We previously examined the needs of the new Afrikan man and woman. The new Afrikan child has specific needs that must be met if they are to develop a healthy sense of themselves and what is possible for them. Our children must be taught that the post-Pride mentality represents a minor facet of the Afrikan experience. They need more than the occasional Black History Month assembly at school. Parents must take it upon themselves to show our young people that there is much more to being Black than calling ourselves niggas and filling up the penitentiaries. We must make a regular practice of purchasing educational DVDs, games, and books that teach our heritage. Black children should know all about Herto, Ethiopia, where the oldest human fossil was found. Tell them about the trek our people made from the crown of Afrika to every continent, spreading the gift of humanity to all corners of the globe. Teach our babies about the pyramids in the Congo Basin and the ancient kingdoms of the Hausa and the Songhai. Do not let them grow up without having learned about Osman dan Fodio, Agaja Trudo, and Askia Mohammed. Tell Black children that Benjamin Banneker was born a slave on a plantation, but in 1753 he invented a wooden clock that kept accurate time for more than 50 years. Tell them that his education consisted of drawings he made of a broken pocket-watch. Black children should be taught about Louis Armstrong, Stevie Wonder, Florence Mills, and Marian Anderson, the first Afrikan person to sing opera at the Metropolitan Theatre. There is no shortage of books written especially for Black children. Black parents can also teach self-reliance to our young people by supporting Black-owned bookstores. BlackBooksGalore.com was established in 1992 by three Afrikan mothers, Toni Trent Parkers, Sheila Foster, and Donna Rand. These enterprising sisters are also talented writers and purveyors of Black literature. They offer books that celebrate Black fatherhood, explore the history of Afrikan-American music, and convey the biographies of notable Afrikan heroes in language that children can understand. BlackBooksGalore.com also carries an array of Continental Afrikan and Caribbean-focused literature, including *The Night Has Ears*, a collection of Afrikan proverbs compiled by Ashley Ryan. Other online bookstores, such as HakimsBookstore.com are excellent sources for children's reading material.

Black parents must stay involved with their schools and in contact with their teachers. Single or disadvantaged parents have a responsibility to seek out mentors for their children, particularly in their teen years. 100 Black Men is a nationwide service organization. Mentorship is just one of their activities. The 100 Black Men Chapter of Oakland, California works closely with the Oakland Unified School District. Their members regularly visit campuses, providing tutoring and positive motivation to our little brothers and sisters. For most of the teenagers, this is their only opportunity to receive that kind of attention. The Oakland Chapter also provides scholarships to high school seniors. The winners are announced each December at the Annual Christmas Kwanzaa Awards Dinner. "Don't Fall Down in the Hood" is a nonprofit organization run by the Institute for the Development of African American Youth in Philadelphia. It was founded by Archye Leacock, who also runs a college-prep program for Black teenagers. Don't Fall Down in the Hood promotes education and stresses the importance of nonviolent resolutions to conflicts. The group visits funeral parlors to impress the horrors of genocide upon young Afrikan people. By 2006, 400 teenage boys had completed the program as part of a court-ordered first-time offenders plan. Only 68 have found themselves in trouble with the law again.

Afrikan people have a choice. We can raise our children or abandon them to a culture that is every bit as bloodthirsty as that of ancient Rome. Will we teach them love of self and kind? Or will we cheer as our children murder one another and then dance to songs written about it? Black teenagers were brought to the West to be niggas, to be abused, exploited, and despised. Parents must teach our children to want more for themselves. Simply saying "stay in school" is the wrong approach. That would be like someone from the 18th century trying to convince us that we should ride horses instead of driving cars. Education is a slow horse. Many of our young people find it difficult, and boring. Dope is a fast car. Being a stripper, prostitute, or gang banger puts our teenagers in the driver's seat. As long as they believe that they are niggas, they will only be interested in slave foolishness. Our children are taught in school that white men created this country. They are told that white men invented everything on Earth. They are told the outrageous lie that white men set us free in the United States, even though we all know that the Emancipation Proclamation was not worth the spit it would take to curse it[25]. Black parents are responsible for teaching our children the truth about their history. The media and the schools are only capable of producing more niggas and slaves. Niggas can't pilot space shuttles or walk in space, but Frederick D. Gregory did. Niggas cannot make advances in the field of entomology, but Charles Henry Turner did. Imagine that! He was the son of former slaves, but managed to get a doctorate in zoology. He was the first researcher to prove that insects can not only hear, but distinguish between

25   Slavery continued unabated in places like Maryland, Tennessee and all other slave-holding Union states.

various pitches and tones. These are the Afrikans with whom our children must be taught to identify. So many rappers claim to care about Black youth, but are they teaching them these fascinating facts about our heritage? Not at all. Instead, they persist in suffocating our children's potential by stuffing them into the Willie Lynch mold.

Our inability to reach our young people is due to a language barrier. We do not speak their language and they do not speak ours. Those of us who have never wanted to be thugs simply cannot fathom why anyone would. Our young people, on the other hand, cannot imagine anything else. This is what happens when they are permitted to waste their young lives playing violent, racist video games and imitating the slaves on television. Hip hop culture does not encourage them to learn, grow, or mature. It simply teaches them to do the same ridiculous Sambo Shuffle as the slave with the mic in his hand. After all of these years of hearing the United Negro College Fund's motto, we finally understand. A mind truly *is* a terrible thing to waste. But before a mind can be filled with facts and figures, it must be given a solid identity. Our children must know where they fit in among all of the facts and figures. They must know their place in the world. We cannot climb the mountain unless we know which way is up. Post-pride culture teaches that up is down and vice versa. It promotes the belief that the quintessential Black man is a nigga who murders his own people and abandons his children. Little girls now believe that the essence of a Black woman is in her ability to bounce her backside, lie on her back, and trick men into buying her things.

CHAPTER FIVE

Rap and Sexuality: Let the Sideshow Begin

"The ruin of a nation begins in the homes of its people."
—Ashanti proverb

"You must use the female against the male, and the male against the female."
—From the Willie Lynch Letter

Afrikans memorialize the sacred through acts of ritual. Each ceremony has a unique and meaningful origin. Ancient Afrikans of the Congo found great relief from their nomadic lifestyles in the discovery of agriculture. It gave them food during the times when their herds were thin. There was a surplus that could be traded with others or stored away for leaner times. Agriculture spurred the first blacksmiths in Afrika to work with iron. They replaced the ancient wooden digging tools with metal hoes and modernized the army's weaponry. For those reasons, our ancestors believed that agriculture was Divine. They ritualized every aspect of the process from the purchase of seeds to the harvest itself. There were several hundreds of ethnic groups in West Afrika. Each had its own way of celebrating agriculture, but all of these ceremonies had one thing in common. The ceremonies all involved singing and dancing. The movements of the dancers often mimicked those of a person laboring in the field. They moved their arms as if they were weeding their yam fields. They shuffled their feet as if they were wading through a swampy area to gather their plantains. Afrikan American slaves continued this tradition. They sang and stomped out a rhythm with their feet as they worked. It lifted their spirits. Many Afrikan Americans are embarrassed by the thought of our captive ancestors dancing and singing in the fields under Florida's brutal summer sun. They consider it proof that the slaves were simple-minded; that they enjoyed the violence and degradation of servitude. This is because they have no knowledge of our culture. One immediately learns that nothing is at it seems in the Afrikan world. Everything in Afrika is a veil for something else. What appears to be a withered piece of wood is actually a snake. A smooth, gray rock in a lake quickly becomes a hippo's rump. At Dogon funerals, the grieving widow sings a song about a colony of ants. Whenever an Ndembu (Zambia) misses his deceased relative, he attaches a piece of white clay to a certain type of tree. This may sound strange to an outsider. But double-meaning and irony are major themes in Afrikan oral traditions. This is part of the reason that we make such great comedians. Afrikan people have cherished the notion of the "trickster" for thousands of years. Long before the West produced Bugs Bunny, the Ashanti told funny stories about Ananse the Spider. The Fon people delighted in the comedic adventures of Legba. For the Yoruba, it was Legba and Eshu. What makes these tricksters so heroic is their ability to always come out on top. At times, it may appear that they have been outwitted and captured. It may seem as if all is lost. But in the end, the trickster always has the last laugh. Thus, our enslaved ancestors were not celebrating their captivity when they danced and sang. They were defying their captors. Despite their every effort, the slave owners could not stop our people from practicing Afrikan culture. Afrikans ritualize work! Our ancestors risked unspeakable retribution so that they could preserve this aspect of Afrikan livelihood. This custom continues today. Sometimes it seems that we just can't get going unless we have some music playing. We sing while we wash the dishes. We turn on our mp3 player or set up a playlist on the computer before we start our chores.

Afrikans also ritualize sexuality. Our ancestors considered it a natural and healthy part of life. Sexual power was important because of its links with fertility and the survival of the group. Afrikan men and women swing our hips and shake to the beat because the power of sexual energy sets us free. Through it, we come to know many of the mysteries of creation and rebirth. Sexual power actually allows us to see through time. What else is a woman looking at when she gazes upon her great-grandchildren if not the future? Our ancestors were not scandalized by dances whose movements suggested the sexual experience. The same concept that helped them become successful agriculturalists also gave them the freedom to express themselves as sensual beings. They understood that there is a time, a season, and a method for everything. They had to know what to plant and when. They also had to know *how* to plant. Our forebears were not circus freaks. Their sex lives were not on display for the entire village. It is clear from their lyrics and videos that a worldwide sexual display is precisely what modern slaves love. This is not an examination of the various artists' styles. Who the best rapper or R&B entertainer is does not concern us. We refer only to the content of their lyrics and/or videos. We are interested in what they say, not how well they say it. Modern slave culture has a devastating effect on the ways that we form families -the building blocks of any community. Our ideas about sexuality will determine whether or not the Afrikan race survives. It is for these reasons that we dedicate an entire chapter to the subject. We begin with a brief overview of the ingredients that make up the Post-pride definition of manhood.

Little Afrikan Boys

The conditions under which the vast majority of today's brothers grow up present numerous challenges to their sense of masculinity. Many grow up in poverty. Poor people are treated with less respect than those from the middle or upper classes. Store owners in underdeveloped neighborhoods treat their customers like subordinates. Arab and Asian shopkeepers bark, "You buy! And then you go out!" at young Black boys. Poor people are constantly being followed through the aisles and accused of shoplifting. Millionaire executives and even movie stars (as we learned from Winona Ryder's 2002 shoplifting conviction) routinely steal from other people. Congressmen and Senators are frequently caught stealing or misusing millions of dollars in public funds. Yet they are not told "only two customers at a time" and their bags are not searched in the stores. Being poor means only being able to live in areas where other poor people live. These neighborhoods are often dangerous and unkempt. In public housing projects, the Housing Authority can burst in at any moment. They can tell us who we can invite into our homes and what we can do inside them. Home owners can demand that a warrant be presented before allowing the police to enter. But the Housing Authority kicks down doors, forces everyone inside to the floor, and destroys the house under the guise of searching for drugs or wanted persons. There is nothing our young brothers can do except watch. Homes in impoverished communities are burglarized more often than those in the suburbs. Anything that does not get stolen is at risk of being defaced. There is very little respect for personal property in the inner cities. Our cars are vandalized with scratches or graffiti. People literally peel paint off of walls and rip down posters in our neighborhoods.

Young Afrikan men learn very early in life that there are no ramifications for any violence committed against them. If their mothers' boyfriends abuse them, no one comes to the rescue. Groups of children in their neighborhoods or schools bully them. They are "jumped", beaten, and robbed. The police viciously beat and murder Black people right in their own neighborhoods and there are no consequences. In 2000, Amadou Diallo was murdered by New York City police officers. He was shot 19 times for reaching for his wallet after being asked to stop and identify himself. The cops were acquitted in court. In 2001, Cincinnati police murdered 19-year old Timothy Thomas. Not one of them was convicted. In 2003, police in Benton Harbor, Michigan shot Terrance Shurn to death. They were acquitted by an all white jury. And in 2006, Frank Jude was viciously beaten by racist white cops in Milwaukee. The cops spread his legs and kicked him in the groin so hard that he had to be catheterized because he was unable to urinate through his penis. A red ball-point pen was jammed into both of his ears and his face was beyond recognition. An all white jury acquitted them as well. Our young men feel that there is no protection for them, and that alone, they cannot protect themselves. Rappers often express this sentiment, making references to the abuse they suffered at the hands of their mother's boyfriends, the police, and other Black men in the streets. LL Cool J's *Father* is one example. It is therefore logical that our young brothers would band together in gangs for the sake of their own security.

Brothers also join and form gangs to get respect from their peers. Even the poorest children make fun of others. If they can find someone who lives under worse conditions than they, the poorer child will be ridiculed and harassed to no end. Our unconscious brothers get into gangs for attention from girls as well. Rappers often talk about the difference in the way that women treated them when they were ordinary citizens in the hood and after they became rich. This is a reality for millions of young Afrikan men worldwide. They see how the girls fawn over well-dressed boys with designer cologne, the latest athletic shoes, and jewelry. Their pride is challenged when they are laughed at or ignored altogether simply because they do not dress in expensive labels. Thus, the early years of many Black men's lives are marked by poverty, violence, lack of protection, and a tremendous lack of regard for their safety, health, or their feelings. These inequalities inform their definition of manhood. For many, being a man means finally having the power to inflict pain or loss on others in a meaningful way. It means finally getting a chance to do unto others what has been done to them. Manhood is payback time.

For Black men, life in the United Kingdom, the United States, South America, and the Caribbean has been one struggle after another. But we managed to stay afloat despite all of our difficulties. We had a safe harbor, a port in the storm. We had the Black community. There was a place where we could be men, where our word counted and our opinions were sought. There was a place where we could assert ourselves and defend our property. We could tell people not to walk on our grass and not to sit on our cars. Children would instantly freeze if older brothers told them to get off of the fence or to stop fighting. When we asked our neighbors to turn their music down, they apologized and complied right away. At the heart of this community was the Black family. The strength and solidarity of Black families is legendary. However large or small, there was always someone- a wise grandmother, a strong uncle, a watchful older sister-someone was there to be a source of comfort and stability. From the time that we emancipated ourselves through the end of the Civil Rights Era, the strength of our families radiated an aura of unity, dignity, order, and respect. We were certain of our friends because our mothers knew their mothers. Our families knew their families. It was common knowledge that we neither appreciated nor would we tolerate disrespect in our own neighborhoods. The most valuable gift that our community gave us was relief from fear. We watched over one another. A young brother did not worry about violence escalating to the level to which we are presently accustomed. Someone would break up the fight. Perhaps it was a cousin or a neighbor. Sometimes it wouldn't be anyone we knew personally. Before the post-Pride era, it was enough for a Black man to have gone to school with our older brother or worked at the Post Office with one of our aunts.

Our young brothers are faced with a daunting task. Even with all of the challenges that many face very early in life, they must somehow go out into the world and function as men. They must pull together all the threads of their experiences and come up with some sense of identity. It is obvious that popular culture fills this void for many brothers. The way that they dress, speak, and behave is right out a rap song. Young Black men end up suspended from school and thrown into jail simply because they want to act like their rap superheroes. They do what the niggas do, regardless of how stupid and destructive the activity. "Real" niggas, according to the slaves, tote weapons, sell dope, and pimp women. One does not join the ranks of "real niggas" without destroying Black families with drugs or shooting Black people. The true measure of a nigga is his capacity for genocide and brutality. This is the premise of the post-Pride masculine persona.

The Three-Pronged Attack on Black Families

During the Civil Rights Movement, the oppressors took note of the source of our strength. They decided to put a stop to that "Black Unity" business. What followed was a massive assault on the Black family, both in the Diasporas and on the Continent herself. Feminists flooded into West Afrika, stirring up discord between the men and women. They introduced competitiveness between the sexes where none had previously existed. In the West, the Black family was attacked with drugs, welfare, institutional sabotage, and the so-called justice system. The CIA distributed crack, heroin, and other narcotics in Los Angeles and New Orleans for the express purpose of turning Black people into the walking dead. The fact that it also turned Black men into ruthless killers only sweetened the deal. Drugs destroyed the trust in many Black families. Dope addicts are constantly lying and double-crossing their own relatives. Afrikan children are often victims of theft by crackhead. By the time they are 7 or 8 years old, these poor Black children have entire lines of credit that were secured by the illegal use of their social security numbers. These credit cards are then used for cash advances to feed the addict's sickness. Little black girls come home to find their piggy banks smashed and all the money missing. Our little brothers' video games mysteriously disappear whenever a dope fiend relative comes to visit. Whatever respect the family had for the addict quickly dissipates after years of watching them walk around in their own filth with dried up, sour-smelling spittle in the corners of their mouths and lint balls in their dirty hair. Having watched them humiliate themselves for a few dollars and hearing rumors of male dope fiends providing oral sex for other men in exchange for five or ten dollars, we can no longer revere or admire these relatives. Drugs bring tremendous violence to Afrikan families. Our lives are torn apart by turf wars and robberies. Though the Post-Pride set touts drug sales as a quick way out of poverty, dope actually contributes to the poverty in Black neighborhoods. Substance addiction is not a static condition. It continues to grow and consume more and more of the family's resources. Addicted parents will even pawn their children's medical equipment such as electric wheelchairs. They will also sell or trade away all of the prescription medications in the house. Dope teaches our children to distrust all Black people, beginning with their own relatives.

First of da Month

Despite the temporary relief it offers to impoverished families, welfare's contribution to Black society has been the removal of men from our families. For decades, poverty-stricken women could not qualify for aid if there was a man in the house. It forced many sisters to choose between living on the streets with no food and raising her children alone. Recent changes to this law, including the laughable "marriage incentive", do nothing to help stabilize Black families. Any couple that marries for a one-time $700 bonus check will likely be divorcing soon. Welfare breeds dependency in Black families. It becomes multi-generational. Our children see their mothers and fathers being paid not to work and come to believe that work is optional. Some think it is ridiculous to work when all they have to do is walk to the mailbox and retrieve a check like their mothers. Welfare is a bad idea and a trap. It would be less expensive and more effective to put these undereducated men and women through training programs so that they will be qualified for the kinds of jobs that they need in order to support themselves. That would alleviate the poverty in our communities a lot faster than passing out butter, cheese, and a few dollars every month. Welfare recipients can be trained as carpenters, plumbers, nurses, caregivers, beauticians, etc. As it stands, this system merely teaches entire Black families to crawl on their knees and grovel. Institutional sabotage was the racist's answer to the gains of the Civil Rights Era. Twisting quotas and taking narrow interpretations of employment and educational law allowed them to maintain the status quo in the West while giving the appearance of progress.

Click-click!

Prisons are another weapon used by the establishment to destroy Afrikan families. Black people are sent to prison for ridiculous lengths of time in disproportionate numbers wherever we live. In the United Kingdom, Afrikan people only make up 2% of the population. Yet we make up 12% of the prison population. Only 12% of the United States' population is Afrikan, yet we comprise 43.9% of US prisoners[26]. We serve longer sentences in prison and jail than our Caucasian counterparts and are subject to more restrictions once out on probation or parole. This keeps our men away from the community. And although in some cases, we are better off without them, thousands of brothers with potential are rotting away in prison for the same

26   Department of Justice, Bureau of Justice: Prison and Jail Inmates at Midyear 2002.

crimes for which Caucasians merely get probation or time in the county jail.

Fatherhood as Rite of Passage for Natural Afrikan Men

The slave's abandonment of his family is what ultimately made these state-sponsored incursions into the Black family possible. In 1970, 38% of Black children in the United States were born to single mothers. In 2005, the figure is a shameful 69%[27]. Mainstream rap is the voice of young brothers under any combination of the aforementioned circumstances. Black fatherhood is rarely celebrated in popular culture. While Caucasian country singers write songs about working to take care of their wives and children, Sambos find new, cute ways to say, "I ain't your baby daddy". Black fathers are not extinct in the West. But when our culture is in the toilet, it is difficult to see over the rim. We do not see the legions of loving, attentive Black fathers that work hard to take care of their children. No one sings their praises, not even the minstrels in hip hop that claim to be so knowledgeable and pro-Black. Fortunately there is more to Black father than what is suggested by intellectually deficient rappers. Far from a coward, the natural Afrikan man distinguishes himself by celebrating the gift of responsibility. Ebony Magazine's celebration of Black fathers in New York (2002) drew a crowd of more than 1,400 people. Honorees represented Black men from all walks of life, from clergymen to celebrities. Mario Van Peebles spoke about his father Marvin. Marvin Van Peebles spoke several languages and taught his children about the stock market at the dinner table. The Reverend Dr. Clarence Norman of First Baptist Church of Crown Heights also received an award. He has worked in

---

27   US Department of Commerce, Bureau of the Census.

the ministry for more than 49 years. Dr. Norman went from being a day care center director to Program Specialist for the US Department of Agriculture. He is also a father of five. The Circle Association also hosts an Annual Fatherhood and Family Celebration in New York. They focus on enhancing Black male-female relationships and helping brothers to accept and fulfill the responsibilities of fatherhood. Brothers in the Caribbean are also doing their part to promote responsible fathering. Fathers Incorporated was established in 1991 by Jamaican men. Their goal is to encourage and support Black men in their quest to become better parents. In recent years, they launched Jamaica's first Father's Day concert.

Weak Slaves Dream of Being Kept Like Mistresses

The modern slave has no problems allowing a woman to feed, clothe and shelter him. But in ghetto culture, it is considered unmanly for him to do the same for her. He would be a sucker. Black men expect women to take care of them without offering any support or even fidelity in return. They do not offer their women any protection. The post-Pride brother finds it amusing when his woman has sexual relations with his friends. He raps about it all the time. He encourages Black women to "let the homies have some", to "let the niggas all swarm (crawl all over her like a horde of wasps)". We cannot imagine that men in Afrika, Asia, or the Middle East would welcome such disrespect into their lives. We do not even find this type of lunacy among male lions, zebras, or owls. Any one of these animals will not hesitate to protect their mates and their offspring. It is unfortunate that so many men today have less sense than animals that lick their own anuses and defecate while they walk. In the days of our physical captivity, the

Black man's soul was aflame with fury each time the inbred, lice-headed captor took liberties with his wife or daughter. Today's slaves gleefully give up all control. They care nothing for their mothers, sisters, girlfriends or wives. The only things worth fighting for are dope, money, shoes, and gold chains.

Ghetto Love (also known as "thug passion")

The term "ghetto" is currently used in two ways. It expresses poor quality (what people who live in poor places can afford). It also refers to stereotypical behavior, that which is similar to racist cartoons. Gold teeth, gaudy jewelry, boat-sized luxury automobiles are popular examples of ghetto culture. What then do today's slaves mean when they use the word "ghetto" to describe love? Are the emotions of low-income Black people somehow different or inferior to those of others? According to mainstream rappers, yes they are! "Ghetto love" involves no courtship. Listen to the lyrics of modern hip hop. The slave's initial contact with the woman involves requests for sex and is peppered with vulgar comments about her breasts and backside. They provide vivid descriptions of their sexual organs and various sexual positions. This is all that today's slave has to offer our sisters. Black women are not living, thinking, feeling human beings in today's rap music. They are merely breasts, lips, and vaginas. There is nothing loving or sacred about the acts described in their lyrics. They merely put our sex lives on display for the entire world. They besmirch the global reputation of Afrikan women. They arouse the curiosity of men from outside our race as well. Caucasian men have always lusted after the Black woman's body. They have always projected their own animalistic desires onto our sisters- describing our women as lewd and filthy because of what was in their own minds.

But today's niggas have taken this a step further. They have thrown the doors wide open. They have invited every man with a pulse to ogle, fondle, and otherwise interfere with our women. Black men have told the world that our women are whores. The world believes us. After all, we should know. It is for this reason that wealthy Caucasian college students and businessmen frequently request Black strippers. They do not hire them out of appreciation for Black features or because they are good dancers. They hire them because they have been told over and over by Black men that our women are bitches and nasty hoes. Our sisters are hookers who will bend over and make their butt cheeks clap for a dollar. In the minds of these college students and businessmen, this also means that they will provide sexual favors after the show.

The confusion about love that exists among Black men is further evidence of cultural neglect. One need only scratch the surface of our history to learn that the Black man is synonymous with masculinity and is the picture of romance. Who can express love like the Black man? Who is there that can sing about love like Luther Vandross, Peabo Bryson, Nat King Cole, or Stevie Wonder? The Post-pride generation sings and raps about love. But their definition of love does not include commitment and responsibility. It is for this reason that the R&B tunes we rave about today will be forgotten by next year. Anita Baker's *Sweet Love* and George Benson's *Masquerade* are still on the radio decades after their release. Slave music sounds like Afrikan music. But when we peer beneath the sound, we find that it is not Afrikan music at all. It is empty. It does not sustain the kind of love that our men, women, and children deserve today. The Afrikan community has absolutely no use for the drug-induced encounters in cars, restrooms at clubs, and Mama's house that are the subject of today's slave love songs. We suffer every day as a result of these irresponsible encounters. Ghetto love is not real love. The only love that has any value to Black people is the kind that creates a loving, nurturing atmosphere in our homes. Black children deserve to be born into stable, committed families. Black men deserve the honest and faithful love of a decent woman who encourages and participates in his efforts to improve both their lives. We do not deserve to be tricked into marriage or fatherhood by greedy women that are too lazy to pay their own bills. Afrikan women do not deserve to be treated like sexual savages. They deserve husbands with jobs and health insurance! The fools of hip hop say that they show how much they love our sisters by "hitting it from the back". *What's in it for the Black community?* These foolish R&B slaves are singing about *nothing* if their lyrics do not teach or inspire us to love one another in the way that we as a people deserve to be loved. Slaves prefer the Eurocentric definition of love. They fall in lust at first sight and proceed to be as reckless and foolish as Romeo and Juliet. Black music is more than the ramblings of angry, violent slaves. For centuries, we have used our voices to paint pictures of hope and solidarity. But that was when we were singing about Afrikan love. Today, we are drowning in thug passion and relations between Black men and women are at an all-time low. Only 41% of Black families in the United States consist of married couples.

No Way Out?

Slave culture spits in the face of Afrikan thinkers such as Frederick Douglass, Patrice Lumumba, Marcus Garvey, Frank John Tennyson Lee (South Afrika), Amos N. Wilson,

President Julius Nyere (Tanzania), and Malcolm X. Rappers have no excuse for their mental stagnation. They have ample resources. They have the opportunity to travel and learn more than what was parceled out to us in substandard schools. It may come as a surprise that many of these rappers actually write beautiful poetry. The beauty does not transfer to their rap lyrics, however. These brothers have seen, heard, and felt things that many of us cannot imagine. They know what is happening in the streets. They have their finger on the pulse of the hood. And the best they can do when they pick up a microphone is say "I shoot niggas". We do not accept the worn-out excuse that they are "caught up in the game and can't get out". Urban Youth Conservation is a gang diversion program based in Minneapolis, Minnesota. It was founded by Ferome Brown and Jimmy Stanback, both of whom are former long-term gang members. Ferome Brown was shot 13 times as a gang member. Now he dedicates his life to saving our little brothers. Urban Youth Conservation outreach workers canvas the neighborhoods, speaking with Black teens and inviting them to come to the center. These brothers give our children a chance to spend time in an atmosphere with positive Black men who know the streets and are fit to be role models. One year after its debut, more than 200 teenagers are signed up for their various activities which include mentoring, tutoring, and sports programs. Urban Youth Conservation was one of the sponsors of Project Cease Fire, a gun buy-back event that took place in February of 2005. The African American Men's Project spearheaded the campaign, bringing together 30 community organizations. Members of the community (some of whom were children) were paid $50 for revolvers and $75 for automatic weapons. Our brothers took 223 guns off of the Minneapolis streets- 25% of the guns that the Minneapolis police confiscate on an annual basis. The event was subtitled "Walking the Earth like Brothers" and was timed to coincide with Black History Month. Millions of young Black men are in need of this kind of guidance, but they have been taught to love and admire niggas. Black men who organize in nonviolent ways for the good of our community are not "real" enough for them.

Reality Shows: The Coons' Nest

We previously noted the ways in which the slave-catchers of R&B and hip hop work to demoralize the Black man, woman, and child individually. The advent of family-themed reality shows allows these saggy-trousered ignoramuses to wrap their filthy tentacles around the Black family. The family-themed reality show is a convenient way to indoctrinate the whole family into the Willie Lynch program all at once. We will leave aside the fact that reality programming is voyeuristic by design and therefore absolutely inappropriate for family situations. We will simply note in passing that no responsible parent would throw their innocent, impressionable and vulnerable babies to the wolves in the media. From the community's perspective, the most dangerous aspect of family-centered reality shows is that they cast slaves and slave-catchers in leadership roles.

These shows are a circus of materialistic slaves happily perpetuating the Willie Lynch program. The Black father is an ATM machine. He is not a teacher or transmitter of history and culture. In fact, he does not make the slightest effort to connect his children with the culture that paved the way for his success. He promotes laziness among Black children by demonstrating that they must beg other people in order to get the things that they want. The reality show father imagines that he is showing the world what a wonderful parent he is by continuously supplying the children with expensive toys and gadgets. He is mistaken. What he is actually doing is stoking the flames of greed and materialism in his children's hearts. He is teaching them two rancid lies about life. They learn that happiness can be bought and that it cannot exist in the absence of luxury. But a father is not an open wallet. A father's job is to protect, provide for, nurture, and educate his family. Our concerns cannot be dismissed as mere jealousy over other people's success. Our question as we observe this slave farce is simply this: *What's in it for the Black community?*

Allowing the slaves that feature in these festivals of ignorance to define our notion of family endangers the Black community. We are creating a generation of lazy and greedy people. We are playing into the stereotype that we are child-like and easily appeased. We also run the risk of creating yet another generation of consumers who produce nothing. This is the reason that all of our money leaves the Black community on a one-way trip. We must teach our children to stand on their own two feet. Many of us attended college alongside wealthy Jewish students. These young people had mothers that were doctors and fathers who worked as chemical engineers. Yet they held summer jobs just like the rest of us. They drove old cars because their doctor and engineer parents expected them to pay for their own transportation. Those Jewish students went on to graduate and obtain advanced degrees. They now own medical pavilions where they employ other Jewish doctors and scientists. *What's in it for the Jewish community?* They have created high-paying jobs for their people. They have improved the general health of the local Jewish community by providing more doctors. They have spread goodwill among their people because they came into the communities to build and improve. President Obama is the perfect example for what we can produce if we turn our backs on this slave foolishness and teach our children to be real men and women. We all laughed when we saw the poor conditions under which Obama lived as a young man. His apartment was old and falling apart. Was he a "nobody" because he did not drive a luxury car with candy paint and glimmering rims? Did he need $200 jeans and alligator shoes to become President?

The Black mother on reality shows is an embodiment of Willie Lynch values. She is petty and materialistic. She reinforces the stereotype that it is easy to buy Black women with a few shiny tokens. She betrays her daughters by indoctrinating them into the hypersexuality of Post-Pride culture. The idea that any Black woman would allow her daughter to be filmed in "bedtime" scenes wearing a full face of make-up and pajamas is appalling. In an age where sick people take the most innocent of gestures as an invitation to abduct and molest children, what kind of mother would allow the entire country into her child's bedroom? The reality show mother is also helping to produce the next generation of slaves and slave-catchers. Black boys from low income or fatherless families watch these shows with longing in their hearts. They dream of being a child in that family. They wish they had all of the extravagant possessions that so-and-so's children have. Since they do not have parents that are able to buy these things, they steal. They get guns and commit robberies. They sell dope as a fast way to make money. Little Black girls watch these programs and are bitten by the greed bug. Many steal to get the things that they want. Some sell drugs. And because they have been taught to dress and behave like whores, many also sell their innocence. It is both disgusting and infuriating when we see 13 year-old girls walking the streets. Yet it has become customary in cities such as Oakland, Little Rock, and Atlanta.

HIV: Three Letters from the Penitentiary

When taken individually, the elements of irresponsibility, irrationality, and the desire to look "cute" and flashy are merely evidence of immaturity. But when we combine these traits with incarceration and a disdain for women, we understand why the health of the entire Afrikan community is hanging in the balance. It is easy to identify the source of the high HIV rates among heterosexual Black women. Intravenous drug users account for only 16% of our sisters who are afflicted with HIV[28]. 81% of infected Black women contracted the disease through sexual contact. Contact with whom? Let us consider the rate at which Black men are incarcerated in the United States alone. The Census Department reports a 2004 figure of 4,919 out of every 100,000 Black men. When the US Department of Justice conducted a study of HIV infection among incarcerated men, they found 1 out of every 100 Black men to be infected[29]. We must not imagine that rape is the most common avenue through which HIV is transmitted in prisons and jails. In fact, Drs. Cindy and David Struckman-Johnson of the University of South Dakota conducted a study on the sexual tendencies of incarcerated men in the United States. Their sample was a large group of prisons in the Midwestern States such as

---

28   Center for Disease Control, *HIV Among African Americans* 2003.

29   US Department of Justice: *HIV in Prisons and Jails* December 2004.

Michigan, Oklahoma, Ohio, and Kansas. Their findings were listed in their 2000 report entitled *Sexual Coercion Rates in Seven Midwestern Prison Facilities for Men.* Their study shows that 25% of men report having sexual relations in prison. Only 7% were victims of rape. The remaining 21% participated of their own accord, sometimes using sex as a method of payment for protection. Men also report performing sexual favors for other men in prison for commissary items such as clothing and cigarettes. These men are eventually released from prison. They return to their former lives, often after having engaged in male-to-male sex. They then enter into relationships with women. As a result, heterosexual Black women find themselves infected with HIV and other venereal diseases.

Rappers understand that if brothers wake up, we will no longer buy their slave music. We will not enjoy descriptions of Black on Black violence and the abuse of our women. Nor will we find it funny when they make songs about refusing to support their own children. It is not in their best interests to encourage Black men to change. Slavery exists in our minds. Black men must learn to think for ourselves. We cannot be afraid to read, to gain new perspectives and ideas. We must not be afraid to change, change, and change again. The Black man's ideas brought civilization to this world. We have forgotten the meaning of dignity. Modern slaves live only the life that we were brought here to live- one of violence and broken families. Every time a real Black man speaks out against these half-dead puppets, we are called "haters". What we *hate* is burying 11 and 14-year old girls. What we *hate* is watching our neighborhoods turn into corridors of death. We *hate* the pathetic look of defeat in our brothers' eyes as they mill about on the sidewalks all day, waiting for night to fall so that they can shoot up our blocks and sell drugs.

Factors Contributing to the Post-Pride Definition of Womanhood

Our sisters learn early in life that the Black woman is on her own. Many are raised by single mothers who were also raised by single mothers. In her study entitled *Family Structure and Dependency: Reality Transitions to Female Household Headship*, Sara S. McLanahan found that Black girls who are raised by teen mothers are 7 times more likely to become teen mothers themselves. This also increases the chances that they will live in poverty. Black women who were raised on public assistance are 64% more likely to stay on welfare as adults. Interestingly, researchers at the University of Canterbury in New Zealand and Duke University in North Carolina found that "girls who have distant relationships with their fathers tend to experience puberty earlier in life than those with attentive fathers". Afrikan girls enter physical womanhood at very early ages, completely bereft of the protection or guidance that fathers are supposed to provide. Little Black girls often grow up watching their mother struggle from paycheck to paycheck. Because teen motherhood and lack of paternal support make it difficult for many Afrikan mothers to obtain a college education, they often work the most grueling jobs. Our mothers clean hotel rooms, work as parking attendants, and stand on their feet all day doing customer service jobs. They work in the healthcare industry, lifting heavy patients and cleaning up blood and human waste. They do white collar work in offices that are only slightly better than sweatshops. Our mothers are forced to meet insane quotas or face being discharged. Their work is incredibly taxing, both on the mind and the body. They then have to come home and take charge of their children at the end of their workday. Our women need help. The Post-pride definition of manhood leaves our sisters absolutely naked and out in the cold. The modern slave's job is to impress the sisters with stereotypically gaudy jewelry. He proves his manhood by wearing flashy clothing and a different grill each time he sees her. What little Afrikan girls learn from watching all of this is that the buck stops with Black women. If the children are to be fed, clothed, or sheltered, it is the woman's responsibility. Black men need not concern themselves with whether or not a child eats or has a bed to sleep in at night. Our women learn that they cannot depend on Afrikan men. In fact, many find that the government is more reliable than Black men. Social Services will pay their rent, buy their food, and give them money for clothes and medicine. Many Black men won't even get on a bus and go *meet* their children. When brothers do remain with their children, they often contribute nothing to the household. Many are simply using the woman for shelter, food, and a few dollars from her welfare check or paycheck. Their lives are little more than an extended childhood. Our little sisters also witness a great deal of violence in their early years. Black women experience domestic abuse at a rate of 35% higher than Caucasian females, and 22 times the rate of women of other races[30]. The Institute on Domestic Violence in the African-American Community reports that the number one killer of African-American women ages 15–34 is homicide at the hands of an intimate partner or ex-partner. Little Afrikan girls grow up in the midst of all this. No one steps in to put a stop to it. If any man does come to her rescue, it is most often a White cop who comes to arrest the offending party and place her into a foster home. We find it pathetic that the police- a group known for beating and killing innocent Black men- do more to protect Black children than our own brothers. Grandfathers, uncles, and male cousins stand by and allow the abuse to continue.

---

30   Bureau of Statistics, 2000.

Aside from being neglected by their fathers (and sometimes their mothers), our little sisters face intense pressure from their peers. They get teased about their clothes and their hair. Black children are unfortunately some of the most prolific disseminators of Willie Lynch propaganda. Sisters with short or kinky hair become the butt of every sort of mean joke. Even young boys pressure our girls to straighten their hair with perms. Our girls are called "baldheaded" and "nappy headed". Girls with longer, straighter hair are always chosen over them. This of course is not the fault of the children. Their parents have obviously been teaching them to hate their own people at home. But our women grow up feeling that their hair is ugly without a perm. Most Black women in the West carry this shame all of their lives. Today's she-slaves will argue that they perm their hair out of convenience and fashion. They will claim that they are not the least bit embarrassed about their natural hair. But these women will never go out in public or attend a formal event without their perm or a wig.

Poverty also gives them no opportunity to travel outside of their immediate environment. They are not exposed to other lifestyles and life choices. Everything around little Black girls from the television to the people at schools and in the streets trains them to be hypersexual. Afrikan girls all over the world are allowed to dress like strippers and prostitutes. They are permitted to speak and behave like female rappers or the dancers in rap videos. Post-pride culture runs through their veins, choking their brains and shaping their interests. If we wish to produce a generation of children with higher standards and a strong sense of culture, we must give them different heroines. They should be taught to emulate Oprah Winfrey's business sense and diplomatic style. Little sisters should be taught that Miriam Makeba gave her entire life for her people.

She was loved all over the world. She never called herself a hoe. She never called us niggas. Miriam Makeba spent her career drawing the world's attention to the horrors of South African Apartheid. When apartheid ended, she spent her life confronting racism all over the world. The beloved sister died onstage after performing at a concert to bring reconciliation to a small town in Italy where the Mafia has been targeting and murdering Black people. (This, of course, is the same Mafia worshipped by modern slaves and after which many rappers name themselves.) Our sisters should be taught to imitate Dr. Valerie Thompson's mathematic genius. It is disgraceful that today's little sisters are not exposed to information on these Afrikan luminaries. It is amazing how our young girls manage to get onto the Internet and create raunchy chat profiles and blogs. They could just as easily use the computer as a study aid. Education is not on the post-Pride agenda. Growth is not part of mainstream Black culture. There is no need for thinking, only blind imitation. Black girls are also abandoned by their mothers. Sisters complain that brothers are not men, that we "need to grow up", and so on. But many of our women are not mature themselves. Their priorities are based in the perpetuation of slave culture. Sisters waste money on buying clothing, hair and nails instead of paying their bills or buying things that their children need. Many waste years and years of their lives scheming, dreaming up ways to attract men and then take their money. Men are far more important to many sisters than their own children.

Ready, Set, Hoe!

After being victimized for most of her life, the post-Pride sister decides to come out swinging. Instead of allowing herself to be used and coming up empty-handed, she now uses sex as a bartering tool. Our sisters advertise their bodies on the streets like slaves on an auctioning block. They welcome sexual advances from any man with a gold tooth. In exchange for letting themselves be used, they receive jewelry, clothing, liquor and drugs. They also receive children without fathers to pay child support or provide health insurance. But the gifts don't stop there. Black women also receive HIV from their irresponsible, unconscious sexual escapades. In 2003, Black women counted for 67% of new AIDS cases in the United States. It was the number one killer of Black women aged 25–34 that year, beating out domestic violence. Though Black teenagers only make up 15% of the US teen population, they made up 65% of the new AIDS cases[31]. In the United Kingdom, Continent-born and Jamaican Afrikans made up 50 and 3 percent of the country's 2002 new HIV cases, respectively. Black women's post-Pride behavior has tainted their reputation worldwide. This is different from the myths that previously existed. Before, it was Caucasian and Arab men who promoted the stereotype of the Black woman's lack of respect for her body. Now our own women go out of their way to invite this sort of attention. This begins as young as 8 or 9 years old. Rap videos are like sex slave exhibitions. Our sisters do everything short of putting their feet up in stirrups to show their breasts, buttocks, and crotches from every possible angle. Black women caught up in the post-Pride deathstyle truly believe they have nothing to offer a man while they are fully dressed. No man was interested in them as children. Their fathers, uncles, and cousins failed them. By the time they reach puberty, they have already learned to use the one thing that is guaranteed to get men's attention. Since brothers will not stay around anyway, they feel that they

31   Henry J. Kaiser Foundation: *African Americans and HIV/ AIDS*. February 2005.

might as well see how much we are willing to spend for a chance to have sex with them. This appears to work for many Black women. They dress like strippers and allow themselves to be trampolines for every brother with a nice watch. Everywhere they go, men are attentive and indulgent. The sister thinks that she has finally managed to gain some control over the men in her life. *How could I possibly be a slave*, the post-Pride sister asks, *when men are putting diamonds in my ears, furs on my back, and I'm smoking purple kush? I'm doing what I want to do. I'm not a slave.* Because she does not know her history, she makes the best kind of slave- a contented one. Black women were brought to the West to be sex toys. It was always assumed that the Afrikan woman's body was a 24-hour amusement park for all kinds of men to enjoy. They were brought here to be disrespected. That is exactly what they get from the mentally rotten thugs in their lives. These men buy them diamonds, but pass them around to all of their friends like a joint. A whore wearing diamonds is still a whore. Our hearts break when we consider what their lives could be like if only they had appropriate role models. How many truly brilliant sisters have we lost to this madness? Could there be another Maggie Lena Walker[32], Betty Shabazz, or Edith Sampson[33] in the ghetto right now wasting her mind, body, and spirit in the pursuit of modern slavery?

It is largely the quest for quick and easy money that leads women into this deathstyle. In order to maximize their dividends, sisters must either land a money-making thug or have sex with a series of thugs. These types of sisters have buffet-style sex lives, with different men coming in and out of their homes every night. But dating thugs invites violence

---

32   First female president of a bank in the United States.
33   First Black person to hold an appointment with the North Atlantic Treaty Organization (NATO).

into the home. Our sisters run the risk of being murdered in a drive-by or attacked by other gangstas who are looking for their boyfriends. They also stand a good chance of being robbed, as many sisters are foolish enough to allow their men to stash dope and money in their homes. Dating violent criminals increases a sister's chances of being the victim of domestic violence. It increases the chances that her children will witness violence or become victims. Being victimized does not deter them. The threat of losing their children often only slows them down. They are high off of the post-Pride deathstyle. They love the drama, the drugs, and the sex. They find it cute and funny to whore their way through life. They do not want anything more for themselves or their children. Every decent brother that they meet is eventually run off by their games and attempts to manipulate him. Many sisters continue in the deathstyle simply because they know nothing else. They are just dating the same kinds of men that they saw their Mother choosing. They get the same results that their Mothers did. This keeps the cycle of fatherless children, poverty, and violence in motion.

The New Afrikan Family

Afrikan people are in need of the stability that strong Black women bring to our families. We commend Sister Nisa Islam Muhammad for founding Black Marriage Day in 2003. Instead of celebrating debauchery, Muhammad organized this event to acknowledge the courage that it takes to survive as Black couples today. In 2005, Black Marriage Day events took place in 70 cities across the United States. Couples renewed their vows and recited the Black Marriage Pledge. Several other Black organizations have joined in the fight to save our families.

Healthy African American Families (HAAF) is an organization based in Los Angeles, California. HAAF conducts research in order to improve our diet and the standards of mental health care for our people. The new Afrikan family wants to appear decent and loving to people on the outside. We want to teach our children the importance of being whole on the inside as well. Strong African American Families (SAAF) is a program that works with rural Black youth ages 10–12. They provide anti-drug education. They also offer classes in parenting skills. We have high expectations for the kind of example that the Obamas will be for our young people. Michelle and Barack were committed partners and careful parents to their two young daughters long before he ran for President. Black people have a choice. We can choose to identify with glory or indignity. We can choose loving Black families or houses full of hoes. It would be nothing short of a blessing if mainstream rap would encourage us to make appropriate choices, but ultimately we are responsible for rescuing our families.

CHAPTER SIX

A Slave and His Money

"Both horse and niggers are no good to the economy in the wild or natural state. Both must be broken and tied together for orderly production... For, if we are to sustain our basic economy we must break both of the beasts together, the nigger and the horse."
—From "Let's Make A Slave" By Willie Lynch as published by The Black Arcade Liberation Library; 1970.

"You can be up to your boobies in white satin, with gardenias in your hair and no sugar cane for miles, but you can still be working on a plantation."
—Billie Holiday

We caution the reader against underestimating the depth and value of West Afrikan trickster tales. Far from the primitive narrations described in the annals of European and American anthropologists, they are a wealth of wisdom. These stories reflect our ancestors' quick wit and unique sense of humor. The story of *Eshu's Hat*[34] comes to us from the Yoruba and is at least 500 years old. There are about 6 different versions of the story. Here is one of the latter renditions:

There were once two men who were both friends and neighbors. They were such good friends that they swore

---

34   The story of *Eshu's Hat* contains 6 Essential Truths. Only one of them is discussed in this chapter.

a sacred oath of loyalty to one another. Through it, each would be obliged to offer assistance to the other in times of trouble. These two men lived on the same street. Their houses faced each other on opposite sides of the street. One day, Eshu walked down the street wearing a new hat. The hat was painted red on one side and black on the other. Later, when the men were working in their fields, one of them mentioned that he had just seen Eshu wearing a red hat. His neighbor laughed. "I saw him with my own two eyes! He was wearing a black hat." The two men began to argue. Their voices grew louder and louder. They showered one another with insults. Each threatened the other. Neighbors heard them and tried to intervene, but they were intent on a fight. Soon fists began to fly.

On his way home that evening, Eshu passed down the street where the two best friends lived. The people surrounded him on all sides and began to question him about the color of his new hat. Eshu showed them all how the hat was red on one side and black on the other. Then he began to laugh and dance[35]. He asked the two men, "When you swore your oath to one another, did you forget to reckon with Eshu?"

Anyone expecting a cathartic ending wherein Eshu is somehow punished for his mischief will be disappointed. Afrikan tales reward intelligence and quick wit. Eshu is not blamed for his role in the fight between the two men. In fact, he is worshipped today in Afrika, Cuba, Haiti, the United States, Brazil, and Puerto Rico. Eshu is symbolic of the Life Experience. For many, he is a symbol of the Nature of God. Life is truly an equal opportunity experience. Life sees no difference between

---

35   Eshu's dance is said to mimic the sexual experience. The Yoruba say, "Eshu dances in the manner of a copulating man."

Afrikan and Asian, male and female, rich and poor. Whether we are in financial distress, in the midst of a love triangle, or dealing with weight issues, *none of us will ever be free from our suffering until we learn whatever lesson we are supposed to learn from it.* The "best friends" at the center of the story of *Eshu's Hat* did not know the value of friendship. If the color of a man's hat could bring them to blows, what would happen when the argument was actually over something substantial? These men deserve no sympathy from the Afrikan perspective. They chose to believe in magical oaths instead of simply obeying Universal Law. We reap what we sow. We get what we give. A cake is nothing more than the ingredients that we put in the mixing bowl. The oath in *Eshu's Hat* was taken by two fools. It would never bring anything but mayhem upon those that took it. Foolishness in, foolishness out.

With all of the foolishness in modern hip hop culture, is there any wonder that their economic strategies are also dangerously flawed? Hip hop teaches Black people that success means having jewel-encrusted watches to dangle in front of our brothers' and sisters' faces. These ideas are rooted in a rigid mindset. They do not even realize that they need these expensive toys and jewelry to cover up what they lack spiritually. They hope that when we meet them, we are so overcome with awe of their clothing that we do not notice the fact that they have absolutely no self esteem. We are supposed to be so blinded by their glitter that we fail to see that they do not even respect themselves. Listen to the lyrics of today's gangsta rappers. They talk about how poor they were when they were children. They blame poverty for all of their maladjusted ideas and behavior. It hurts them so very badly to be without expensive shoes and pinky rings! It embarrasses them. They imagine that every person on the streets is judging them. They mistake innocent glances for scornful stares. But no matter how many millions they make, they will always find themselves in the middle of some sort of drama. Foolishness in, foolishness out.

How these popular slaves handle their finances is none of our concern. They earned their money. If they chose to strap their entire life's earnings to a rocket and blast it into space, we would not be affected at all. But the financial mindset expressed in modern rap and R&B lyrics is immensely dangerous to the average Black person and the entire Afrikan community by extension. These notions stand in stark contrast to our cultural values. In fact, they warp the very foundation of the Afrikan identity.

Afrikan people in the West have become extremely wealthy from the hip hop empire. Sylvia Rhone was responsible for Elektra's record $300 million revenue in 1996, and Lebaron Taylor (Senior Vice President of Corporate Affairs for Sony Music Entertainment, Inc.) oversees a $4.7 billion dollar enterprise. Bad Boy Records reported average sales of $80 million over a two-year span alone. From a marketing perspective, Afrikan culture is a proven gold mine. Everything from our singing, dancing, comedy, literature, actors, culinary arts, and fashion has worldwide appeal. The world danced and sang along with The Supremes and the jazz and blues greats before them. During the Pride era, non-Blacks even put chemicals in their hair to create the Afro effect, wore dashikis and chanted "Down with the Man". The very words that fall from our beautiful lips are pure gold. Ebonics has become so popular and pervasive that it is used in everything from official settings (such as Colin Powell's ill-fated "Don't go there" comment in Ohio - complete with "talk to the hand" gesture) to newscasters remarking that the locals were "getting their groove on" at a free concert on the green.

For these reasons, rap has the potential to soar beyond its present $1.5 billion dollar mark despite the current economic downturn. Rap music is evolving and expanding. There are new styles of rap in the making, with new manners of expression. There are phenomenal rap artists waiting in the wings, brothers and sisters whose intelligence will not permit mere imitation of hip hop's slave of the month. The American Midwest is a hotbed of raw talent. Cleveland, Chicago, and Little Rock could easily become the next capitals of rap music. The Bay Area in California is another wellspring of fresh and original talent. The cities of Vallejo, San Francisco, and Oakland are beaming with men and women who will be the next "big thing". New York, Dallas, North Carolina and Chicago are all teeming with contenders for rap's heavyweight belt. There will be new technology to make clear high-tech beats which in turn will lead to new dances, new hairstyles and trends in fashion. This is what we do. This is our business. Different forms of Afrikan culture have been co-opted by people from many different cultures. But the Afrikan element is inseparable from the authentic product. Rap music is popular in Asia, but the essence of rap is outside of the Asian cultural and historical experience. Latinos also love rap, but rap did not originate in Latino neighborhoods. It was not carried to the West in the hearts and throats of Latino people. Removing the Afrikan-influenced beats and reflections on the cumulative Black experience would result in rap's complete collapse. The Afrikan is the I-beam of hip hop. The mainstream is working very hard to sever it from its Afrikan roots. In so doing, they remove the rich cultural context of Black music. We lose its wisdom, antiquity, and its singularity. We lose its soul.

As rap sales clearly demonstrate, post-Pride behavior can easily be converted to cash. But how does the manufactured identity handle this money? In a word- spend! Ball! Clown! Shine! Floss!

Rap artists are often the first to showcase new jewelry, shoes, suits, etc. Without even trying, they are living advertisements, walking commercials. Flashy clothes and elaborate jewelry are part of the rappers' image. Very few neglect to mention the size of the diamonds in their ears and on their wrists. Rappers are not to be blamed for their love of the exotic and expensive. The average Black person, however, cannot keep up with the ever-expanding cache of trinkets, cars, expensive liquor, and clothing that a multi-millionaire can accumulate. And this is where many of us find ourselves in trouble.

Selling Ourselves

It would have taken too long and cost too many lives for the Europeans to conquer Afrika themselves. It was easier, safer, and much more entertaining for them to simply watch Afrikans do their dirty work for them. So they gave the Afrikans worthless European goods- liquor, cigarettes, and cheap flint rifles and cutlery. They knew about the trifling jealousies and rivalries between the various ethnic groups. They knew that once one group started to dangle their newly acquired possessions in front of other groups' faces, Afrikans would do anything- including murdering and selling other Black people- so that they, too, could have shiny toys and lung cancer. And so it was. At the close of the Civil Rights Era, the oppressors played the same game, only with slightly different rules. They decided to allow a few of us to obtain a handful of shiny things and then watch the rest of us scramble, fight, and kill to get them. As in Afrika, the fighting and killing is overwhelmingly against people of our own race. When segregation ended, internalized racism drove us to make a crazed dash into previously "back door only" stores. Just days before, the owners of these establishments would not permit paying Black customers to use the rest facilities. Yet we swarmed into their stores, drying up Black-owned operations that had provided years of faithful service in the process. In exchange for destroying our own businesses, we got to feel like we were "somebody" every once and a while. We had been granted the grand privilege of strolling into the front door of Caucasian owned businesses and giving them all our money. When we peer into this fog of self-hatred and confusion, we can clearly see Eshu. He is laughing and dancing up a storm over all of this foolishness.

Our addiction to television is an inroad for the oppressor. Black-oriented programming is flooded with advertisements for ridiculously priced cars, jewelry, and athletic shoes. There are more fast food advertisements on BET than Caucasian-oriented channels such as Disney and WB. In 2003, University of Minnesota professor Corliss Wilson Outley led a research team that examined the prevalence of fast food advertising during children's programs. They compared commercial content of afternoon and evening shows on Disney, WB, and "B"ET[36]. Nearly half of the ads were for fast food and sodas. 66% of the fast food commercials were on BET, 34% were on WB. There were no fast food advertisements on the Disney channel. 82% of soft drink ads were on BET, 11% were on the WB network and 6% were on Disney. This enables corporations to get their hooks into our Afrikan minds early in life so that we will grow up to be irresponsible spenders. It gives them a chance to put our minds to sleep, to make us into the unconscious niggas that make them extremely wealthy. Our quest to have the shiny things on television keeps us in debt.

---

36   We question the name "Black Entertainment Television" as most of the material featured is detrimental to the Black psyche and does not represent the interests and values of Afrikan people.

It also gets many of us locked away in prison. The slave mind focuses on window dressing- superficial "improvements" in our lives. Today's slave imagines that he has accomplished something monumental whenever he buys a new watch or pair of shoes. But his social, economic, and employment situation remains just as it was before the new watch. 2-karat diamond earrings on a modern slave are like candy paint on a rusted car with no engine. The West has invested hundreds of years and billions of dollars molding Black people into greedy, desperate, self-hating slaves. This is how "Willie Lynch" dreamed it would be. This is the racist's paradise. For them, it is a win-win deal. They hate us and treat our people like trash. In exchange, we murder each other and give them all of our money. What appears to be a harmless fascination with expensive things is actually a mental return to plantation life. This represents a significant break with our original culture. In Afrika, we were not considered great because of the amount of gold we had or how many servants we employed. What made an Afrikan great was his love for his family and his willingness to share his fortune with those closest to him. He may have been rich in cattle and land, but the first questions out of the mouths of his peers were "How many children do you have?" And "How are your mother, father, and siblings faring?" Our ancestors in the West knew that they had been bought. They realized that they could also be sold again and again. Surely a piece of paper that could be exchanged for an entire human being must hold tremendous powers. Our ancestors watched through deprived eyes as their captors slept on comfortable beds with fine linen. Our people slept on the cold, hard floorboards of the pantries or on mats of straw in the slave quarters. When slavery ended, entire Black families trudged laboriously through rain, snow, and mud, watching

Caucasians speed past in their shiny automobiles. We came to believe that if we also possessed these things, that we would be "somebody". We would be untouchable, free from abuses and deserving of respect or at least, fear. Rappers subscribe to this philosophy. They carry plantation life into the new millennia with their "I have things that you don't. Look at me, I'm *somebody!*" It is unclear how much of this is simply fueled by the capitalist values of the West. But the socio-historical aspects of materialism and consumerism among Blacks must not be overlooked.

At first glance, "slave" hardly seems appropriate for materialistic Black people today. Slaves in 16th century America were perpetually deprived. They never knew the power and convenience of ownership. Today, we drive brand new automobiles off of showroom floors. We dress in fine clothes and eat in fancy restaurants. We are free to come and go as we please. Though many of us are poor, we seem to have plenty of money to spend on the nonessential things we enjoy. How can our economic behavior be connected to slavery? There are several answers to this question. Materialism brings competition. Competition brings more jealousy to our community. We cannot escape the fact that jealous rivalries between West Afrikan ethnic groups facilitated Afrika's demise. To this day, we are like crabs in a barrel, each snapping and scooping up whatever we can in an attempt to look "better" than our own people. Our former captors would be quite pleased to know that 400 years later, they still hold the key to our enslavement. They still know what buttons to push to set us against one another. The mental slavery that grips post-Pride culture is no accident. During the Civil Rights Movement, we demonstrated that we valued each other over material possessions. No sales could make us cross the picket lines. Shop owners tried to entice us with discounts and conspicuous displays in their store windows. But we would not be moved. We were not slaves for the Caucasians and we certainly weren't going to be slaves to fashion. We recognized that though we are all individuals, we had everything to gain from standing together. The CIA and local authorities tried every trick in their bag to stir up discord between the various Civil Rights leaders. Small jealousies surely persisted throughout the Civil Rights Movement, but we knew how foolish it would have been to broadcast them to the entire world.

Black Barbies and Kens

The uncompromising materialism of post-Pride culture stems from a lack of self-esteem. Many Black people still feel that they are nothing without expensive cars, jewelry, and clothes. It is important to remember that many of the behaviors which we decry do not have their roots in rap music or today's R&B. They come from an intense campaign of brainwashing that began centuries ago and that continues in various forms to the present day. Our only hope of conquering this kind of thinking is in maintaining a scientific perspective. Not only must we expose the symptoms of materialism, greed, and the like. We must expose those cultural and historical circumstances that cause us to think this way as well.

Names are sacred to our people. Our ancestors put all of their hopes and dreams for their children in their names. A boy in Nigeria is called "Enitan" because it means "his story is/will be great". Isn't this what we want our sons? Black men want our daughters to know that our love for them is timeless and unconditional. That is why Igbo girls are called "Adannaya" (Daddy's Girl/Father's Daughter). It is not of our culture to make up names that "sound cute" simply for the sake of being different. The ridiculous "ghetto names" that we encounter today represent a break with our traditions.(It is typical of the post-Pride mentality to value hollow "cuteness" over substance. Everything in rap culture is cute on the outside but empty inside.) Like the slave owners before them, the post-Pride generation is wiping out our history. Slave owners sought to erase our history when they took away our names. It was like wiping words from a blackboard. It was their way of erasing everything that we were and everything that we had known prior to being enslaved. Though our captivity has ended, many of us are still branded with the names of the men and women that enslaved and tortured us.

One would think that having to answer to European names would be enough of a reminder of the terrible past. One would think that, having swallowed this bitter pill, we would have had enough of other people's names. But the foolishness of the Black male in rap culture knows no bounds. Whether in a video or on the streets, we find Afrikan men draped in other men's names. These brothers wear the names of designers like teenage girls wear their boyfriends' letterman jackets. The names of other men are constantly falling from their lips. They actually derive their sense of self-worth from the names of other men. Not honorable men such as ancestors, Black pioneers, or Afrikan heroes, but the names of drug-peddling, woman-hating coons that teach Black children to hate themselves. It's as if they want the world to know whose slave they are. When we see a Black man covered in labels, what he is saying is that he is one of [fill in the name of any famous designer]'s niggas. This is why maintaining a scientific perspective is essential. Afrikan people have not recovered from the Western holocaust. We are still suffering. Generation after generation, Black families have struggled with the insecurities, disjointed reasoning, fears, and frustrations of slavery and colonialism. There yet remains that nameless, shapeless maw from which spring the maladjusted antics of unconscious Black men. They have not dealt with their Afrikan selves. It is much easier to just be niggas. It is easier to imagine that we appeared in the West out of nowhere in chains on the shores of America, the UK, or the Caribbean. They would rather identify as niggas which are the creation of racists- and thus as victims- than to be healed through a connection to the people who spared us by bearing the bulk of our pain in the West.

When we accept the European definition of success, we are fighting a losing battle. There will always be the next "big thing". There will always be a more powerful engine, a bigger diamond, and a more exquisite wristwatch. We will waste our lives trying to out-shine one another. Eventually, we will all end up poor and living hand to mouth. We are so busy fighting over shiny toys and flashy clothes that we have gotten distracted from everything else that is going on around us. Empty materialism makes us all very petty people. Consider this, Afrikan people: all of this dope-slinging, robbing, and murdering is over non-essentials. We don't need labels to live. These thugs in the streets are not stealing and killing to buy bread. They are stealing and killing so they can shine! And while we kill and compete with one another, everyone else reaps the benefits of Afrikan resources, culture, and ingenuity. As our people in the Congo say, "While two birds were arguing over a kernel, a third swooped down and carried it off." The truth is that whether we are from Brazil, the Caribbean, or the Continent herself, we are all in the same boat. We must stop judging ourselves and each other based upon how many of Massa's toys we have. Many of us are blind. We think that the toys we gain justify the damage that this greed causes. If we complain that a brother is selling dope, his response is inevitably, "But I drive a [fill in the name of any European or Japanese automobile]". If we complain that a sister is having sex with men for money, she will say, "And I got a mink coat, too!" In and of themselves, they have no value. It's Massa toys that make them who they are. Our initial reaction when we see one another on the streets is to instantly grade the person's hair, clothing, and jewelry and compare them to our own. The moment we see each other, we automatically start playing Willie Lynch's game.

One of the chief aims of any terrorist campaign is making the victims feel helpless. This discourages those who are abused from running away or defending themselves. The Willie Lynch program was no different. There had to be some mechanism in place to subdue the Black masses who often outnumbered Caucasians on the plantations. Our confidence had to be broken. A number of inhumane tactics were employed to achieve this goal. This condition continues to plague our people. How is it that a people capable of generating such incredible revenues remain the poorest wherever we live? We have been blinded by the flash of platinum and clusters of winking diamonds. We recognize the power of money, but we transfer that power right out of our community instead of finally taking complete ownership of our neighborhoods, schools, and entertainment franchises. Just like the money-hungry thugs in rap songs, the people in control of Western nations care not for humanity, religion, nor justice. The West cares about money. If we control the billions of dollars that we generate, we control a part of this nation. Why shouldn't we? Is this not our country as well? Afrikan people would also do well to imitate the business stratagem of other prosperous minority groups. Jewish people patronize Jewish dry cleaners, Jewish doctors, Jewish dentists, and even Jewish auto dealerships. This ensures that their capital circulates throughout their community first before touching the hand of any outsider. The outsiders get the scraps. The choice capital remains under Jewish control. They can depend on one another to keep their businesses afloat. While the Jews must certainly experience hatred and jealousy among themselves, they also realize that their children attend the same schools. They belong to the same professional organizations. They share the same history, goals, and interests. When tensions arise, their sense of self-preservation forbids them from airing their problems before the entire planet. Open displays of infighting do not instill confidence in their customers and business associates. It is bad for business. This is different from the rap world where Black men frequently insult and degrade one another in front of the cameras merely to entertain their Caucasian fans.

Black women have made several innovations in manicure and hair styles, yet both of these markets are dominated by Asians who do not even use these products themselves. Many young women immigrate to the United States from Cambodia, Vietnam, and South Korea solely for the purpose of working in manicure salons in Black neighborhoods. Entire Asian family empires have been built around the synthetic hair and nail businesses. We must ask our sisters why they invent new styles and techniques just to teach Asian women more ways to make money in our neighborhoods. Afrikan people account for more than 30% of the $4 billion annual hair and nail market-over one billion dollars. Our women could go from desk jobs to being wealthy entrepreneurs. They could finally have a chance to give their children all of the things they need. The same is true for hip hop fashion. Everything from jackets and jeans to socks and underwear can be produced by Afrikan-owned firms out of Afrikan-supplied materials. Manufacturing plants could be opened in all 50 states as well as the Caribbean. This would create hundreds of jobs. Afrikan people create trends in all types of clothing, from street wear to business attire. Why do we then rush into the malls and pay top dollar to buy back our own inventions? Why do we create markets for others to dominate? Others use our inventions to make their families independently wealthy for several generations. We, meanwhile, are starving, living in apartments that are on the brink of collapse, often dependent upon the arbitrary and sometimes cruel hand of Social Services- all because we do not know the value of our culture. Instead of doing for self, we rush out every weekend to make sure that Caucasians and Arabs have mansions, yachts, summer homes, private jets, private education for their children, and villas overseas.

Rap artists frequently complain about the stark poverty of the ghettoes, the absent fathers, and the worthless public schools that "don't teach us shit". Yet they hold in their hands the very means by which these injustices may be alleviated. If the schools are failing Black children, why don't we open our own schools? Opening Black schools not only solves the problem of miseducation, it also provides employment for Black architects, construction workers, teachers, nurses, cafeteria workers, bus drivers, and administrators. Why bemoan a situation that is within our power to correct? What is stopping our brothers who clearly recognize the dire need from helping our babies? Nothing holds them back save the invisible chains around their minds. This is not our way of begging. We do not expect rappers to carry the entire race. The truth is that collective struggle brought rap music into existence in the first place. Collective struggle made it possible for rappers to walk the streets today. It was the raising of the collective Black fist that keeps the Caucasians who are suddenly so "down" with "niggas" from stringing us up and setting us afire today. The Post-pride contingent is most ungrateful. Today's modern slaves spend a great deal of time fantasizing about the White women in rap videos and none thinking about the people who made it possible for us to even stand on the same sidewalk as White women without being dragged from our homes and murdered, as was the case with Emmitt Till. These thugs would not be sitting in luxury automobiles or wearing fancy clothes if former generations had not cared enough to break the social and institutional barriers that kept us in poverty. We do not begrudge rap artists their possessions. The music industry is ferocious, and whatever money these brothers make is hard-earned. But we decry the manner in which communalism has taken a back seat to Eurocentric greed and competition. Doing for self and kind is absent from the post-Pride agenda. We have not been holding our collective breath in expectation of any such feat from the rap arena. Brothers and sisters across the United States have taken the initiative for the sake of our children. One such project is the Nubian Village Academy in Virginia. This wonderful organization teaches Black children Afrikan and Western History, Kiswahili, yoga, mathematics, and science. The most fundamental lesson that our children learn at Nubian Village is the concept of doing for self. In a Black-owned school, all of the authority figures are Afrikan. Every problem that arises is solved by Afrikan minds. The notion of self-help is imprinted on their consciousness, and our young Black people learn to be self-sufficient. This is a major step towards mental freedom, yet there is much more to be done. In addition to placing Afrikan schools in all 50 states, we are in need of a stronger and more varied economic infrastructure. Black banks, hotels, and assisted living homes are precisely the types of enterprises that will liberate our people. When we cleanse ourselves of the stench of the post-Pride mentality, we will be able to look beyond the borders of our individual nations and create a pan-Afrikan economy. For example, it is no secret that the Western diet has endangered the health of our people by making them overweight. Where, then, are the Black-owned restaurants that sell healthy foods grown on Black-owned farms in the US, the Caribbean, and Afrika?

There are plenty of opportunities in the rap industry for people of all levels of education and experience. Rap can open doors for Black stockbrokers, attorneys, accountants, fashion designers, architects, photographers, concert promoters, agents, and managers. Hip hop tours alone should be lucrative ventures for Black security staff, pilots, sound and light crews, emergency medical staff, and Afrikan-owned hotels and diners. This would send fresh money flowing throughout the Afrikan community. We must desist from supporting Black-owned labels that do nothing but continue the exploitation of our people. Withholding money gives us more power than spending it. It immediately forces the boycotted company to change its policies in order to protect the bottom line. These Black fashion designers are not making clothes "for us". If they did, they would be reasonably priced. These so-called African American label owners know full well the extent to which keeping up with the Joneses has devastated our community. They also know how hard their own mothers and fathers struggled to put clothes on their backs when they were children. Instead of creating fashionable clothes that the very people from whose culture their fortunes are derived can afford, they set their prices at astronomical levels. They set in motion the spiral of jealousy and desperation that feeds the dragon of Black on Black violence. Instead of putting their stores and factories in our neighborhoods and giving our distinguished Black farmers the opportunity to supply them with materials, they ship their businesses overseas. Black farmers in the US, Afrika, and the Caribbean are just as capable of providing cotton, dyes, and other production materials as those in Asia. But they are passed over by Black people, who then flash their diamonds and show off their possessions on television while Black farms sink deeper into debt. A handful of Afrikans become extremely wealthy and the Black masses pick up the tab. It would be both unfair and untrue were we to claim that Black fashion designers have completely deserted the Afrikan community. For example, Damon Dash of Rocawear has a long and inspiring history of working with urban youth in New York City. He helps provide programs centered on our children's personal growth and development with an emphasis on the importance of recreation.

How can post-Pride Blacks be slaves when they dine on lobster and prawns, use the latest cell phones, and wrap themselves in exotic labels? The answer is that they do the work of slaves. What are we doing when we charge our credit cards to the limit at the mall? Who benefits from our conspicuous consumerism? We are lining the Massa's pockets. We are behaving like slaves. Sadly, there are Black people whose only sense of self-satisfaction comes from how much money they can hand over to Caucasian people. Many misguided Blacks can be heard saying, "This is a $3000 watch" or "My rims cost $1500 apiece." A proper translation of these statements would be "I gave Massa $3000 dollars!" and "Look what I gave Massa! $1500 for each rim!" Rap is in no way responsible for the poverty that persists among Afrikans in the Diasporas and on the Continent. Though at times ignorant and unsettling, rap music does not have the power to devastate a community. It is the mindset cultivated by certain genres of rap music, gangsta rap in particular, which has left our people in the lurch. Afrikan people, do not think for even a moment that the extreme materialism in our community is coincidental. We must not shrug it off as merely a product of capitalism or historical deprivation. The Civil Rights Movement was the modern world's first glimpse of a strong, unified Black people. It was like acid to racist Caucasians, but there was nothing they could do about it because we simply were not afraid of them. Threats of violence and the loss of our jobs could not make us fear them. Fear has been the racist's primary weapon, his most valuable tool for tinkering with both Afrikan and Caucasian people's minds. The oppressors decided that if they could not stop the Movement, they could at least try to profit from it. After all, they only brought us to the West to make money. Being able to molest Black children, rape our women, and torture our brothers was a bonus. The trick they employed was actually a very old one. It worked in Afrika 400 years ago. Because many of us choose to ignore (and therefore, disrespect) our history, it is working today.

The New Afrikan Spender

Despite our ill-advised post-segregation flight from Black-owned establishments, Afrikan people in the United States have been and continue to be successful business owners. Afrikan-owned enterprises netted 32.2 billion dollars between 1987 and 1992 alone[37]. Imagine what we could do today if we increased the number of Afrikan stores and firms? Why patronize cluttered corner stores with ridiculous prices and rude, racist owners who won't put a single dime back into our community when we so desperately need the revenue to build our financial infrastructure? Afrikan people have the tools necessary for repairing the devastation visited upon us by the Western nations. But our money must remain in our communities in order to be of any benefit. The Europeans have taught us that money is the root of all evil. We hear similar nonsense from today's slave rappers. If it wasn't for their desperate need of money, they wouldn't be selling heroin. If it wasn't for all the back child support they owe, they would spend time with their children. It's the *money's fault* that people stoop to subhuman tactics to get it, pimping and murdering others. *Evil* is the root of all evil! Bringing more legitimate dollars into our communities could only make things better. It is our minds that need healing, enlightenment, and expansion. Poverty and unconsciousness go hand in hand. This is the reason that rap's 1.3 billion dollar watershed never trickles down into the hood. Black people must rediscover the concept of community. Our vast intellect and phenomenal talent can easily transform us into financial giants, but we allow volunteer slavery, jealousy, and other trifling emotions to become a barrier between ourselves and financial independence. Together we can do it. We have done it before. How can we stand together

37   US Department of Commerce, Bureau of the Census 1992.

when we praise thugs that preach messages that do nothing but divide us? This attitude is clearly demonstrated in rap lyrics. These gold-plated clowns threaten to beat, kill, and rob us all. Whether millionaires, poor, or out of work, other Black people are the targets of their savagery. It is precisely this type of predatory lunacy that drives Black businesses to close their doors and discourages new companies from bringing jobs to our neighborhoods. The extremely high incidence of Black on Black crime make it abundantly clear that non-Blacks stand a greater chance of prosperity in our neighborhoods than we can hope for ourselves. Why should Afrikan people be afraid that they will be robbed and/or murdered for opening a legal enterprise providing valuable services for their own people? Why should we miss out on our rightful share of the $3.3 trillion dollars that swell the pockets of American businesses owners annually?

Black people must exercise better judgment as to how we use the dollars at our disposal. Black parents must teach our children the value of money by requiring them to do chores in exchange for toys and cash allowances. They must be taught to save money; in piggy banks as small children and in saving accounts in their teen years. Afrikan parents must also spare our children the constant bombardment of advertisements by limiting their television time. Black adults must learn some self-esteem. We need to stop trying to fill the holes in our lives with shiny things. It is ridiculous to believe that a possession makes a person "somebody." Next month, the shoes, jeans, or purse will be out of style and they will be right back to being "nobody" until they find another Caucasian to make rich. We must use the Internet to find Black-owned businesses and keep the revenue circulating among our own people. We must stop cowering like slaves on the sidelines while our culture is being misused in order to line the pockets of non-Blacks and their Black slaves. Our speech, athletic styles, dance, fashion sense, folklore, and inventions are not resplendent examples of Western genius. They are proof of the Afrikan's ability to turn the struggle for freedom and equality into a work of art. These and all elements of rap culture belong to us. Yet Black people nearly break our necks to run out and teach outsiders everything there is to know about being Black. We do not realize that we are giving away our culture for free. We mindlessly explain the use of Ebonics, our modes of dress, and how to perform our dances step by step without asking for a dime in exchange. But if we want to learn the dances of the Caucasians, we know from the outset that we must pay. If we want to learn the tango, it will cost $80 per lesson. If we want to waltz and salsa, the lessons are even more expensive. They realize the value of their culture and are not foolish enough to share it with anyone without compensation. Our teenage brothers and sisters on the schoolyards take off their backpacks and jackets and slowly demonstrate the intricacies of hip hop dance to their Caucasian, Asian, and Latino friends, who later go on to make How To Hip Hop DVDs and open dance classes of their own. Afrikan people, search the Internet for DVDs that offer Black dance instruction. We will be lucky if we find more than 1 Afrikan person on the covers of these products. 95% will feature Caucasians in their "hip hop gear" on the cover (with their hats turned to the side so that we know that they are *really* down).

Rap is not alone in this regard. We find that there is virtually no sector of Black culture in which Caucasians, Latinos, and other non-Blacks have failed to corner the market. Even Afrikan religions such as Ifa/Orisha and Diaspora-based faiths such as

Rastafarianism are overflowing with non-Black opportunists. Caucasians flock to Afrikan bookstores and community activities, looking for a chance to sell us back our own culture. Our examination of Internet websites with information on Ifa/Orisha and Ras Tafari reveals countless instances of dashiki-wearing, dreadlocked, Kente Cloth-wearing outsiders who then go on to charge Black people astronomical amounts of cash for "Afrikan spiritual readings" and "religious initiations". This perpetuates their feelings of superiority and tightens their control over the Black community both spiritually and economically.

It would be impossible for us to list all of the benefits we enjoy thanks to the sacrifices of the Civil Rights Pioneers. We owe it to ourselves and our brave brothers and sisters of the Movement to take a lesson from their vast organizational skills and their solidarity. Black artists, athletes, and entertainers must return to practice of boycotting cities with reputations for racism and racial violence. The Klu Klux Klan proudly displayed a cross in downtown Cincinnati until 2004. It was part of the annual Christmas display. Would this have been the case if Black people had simply stopped shopping there? Would the murderous activities of the Cincinnati police continue to go unchecked if their budgets (and therefore, salary and job opportunities) dried up due to an unequivocal boycott of their entire city? The general Afrikan population can make our voices heard by boycotting television channels where our people are portrayed as living stereotypes, radio stations with racist or post-Pride agendas, and clothing designers who do not invest in the development of the Black community. We can make significant changes simply by withholding our collective billions from those who seek to destroy our sense of self. We must not forget that there are economic incentives to preserving Black culture. One lesson that Black people should have taken away from our centuries of captivity is that no amount of money is worth losing our heritage.

Rap is modern art. It is our culture. It is our tool of liberation and a link to our past. Rap music is one of the ways in which we preserve the tradition of the West Afrikan griot[38]. It is also our antenna. Rap allows us to receive a wide range of perspectives on society, politics, fashion, and even religion. Rap is also our link to the future. We are often able to predict future events by analyzing the current trends. Rap is our Afrikan baby, carried thousands of miles in the bowels of slave ships and incubated in the hearts, minds, and souls of millions of our incredibly strong forebears. Hip hop was weaned in the throats and on the lips of plantation captives, chain gang workers, bebop and blues musicians and in the rhythmic and rhyming sermons issued from the mouths of Black ministers in the churches. As our connection to our roots becomes weaker, so will the quality of rap music. If we continue in our current direction, we will eventually lose this seemingly innate talent. Rap will then become monotonous, empty, and irrelevant to the masses. Fans will turn on hip hop just as they did with disco, and our art will be confined to the annals of history. We will have gained nothing from having behaved like circus freaks for the world. Popular rappers will find themselves rapping jingles for hemorrhoid and age spot ointments just to make ends meet, or they will return to the drug trade and end up with rhyming prayers on their headstones. Once the connection to Afrika is completely

---

38   The West Afrikan griot is the grandfather of rap music. Griots were singers, poets, and historians in the oral traditions of our ancestors. This form of storytelling led to the creation of blues music which is the precursor of rap.

broken, the well will run dry and the world will turn to another ethnic group for authentic cutting-edge music. It therefore serves our cultural and financial interests to preserve rap music while we may.

No amount of charity work is going to improve our collective situation. Our salvation lies in re-thinking our economic behaviors. This includes gaining the education and training necessary to expand our wealth. We must show ourselves to be intelligent people. We must learn to *think*, not just salivate and spend. We must think not only of the price on the sales tag. We must also weigh the spiritual cost of our purchases. We must ask ourselves whether our purchases are based in wisdom and utility or if they only serve to further injure our self-esteem. It also behooves us to ask whose pockets we are filling. Are we helping ourselves when we buy from racist Asian shopkeepers who don't even live in our communities? When our women get their nails done by Asian women who couldn't care less about our people? When our men buy liquor and bootleg movies from Arabs? Why not buy online from our own people? Most importantly, we must never forget our history. We were brought here to make others rich. Amending the Constitution did not change their plan. It only forced them to change their tactics.

Economic Relief for Afrikan People

No one wants to start changing their economic behaviors during a financial crisis. When so many of us have lost our jobs and even our homes, the last thing we need to hear is a lecture about what we should be doing with the limited funds available to us. Following the post-Pride financial model (spend, spend, spend!) is not an option when there is nothing left to spend. The time to plan for financially stressful conditions is now! We do not yet know the full extent of the present economic downturn. This may be difficult to accept. It may improve sharply in the following months. It may linger on for years. Afrikan people were the first to feel the pangs of the recession. But the truth is that millions of our people were already living at or below the poverty line long before the recession was declared. When we find ourselves in desperate situations in life, it is often because we made an appointment to be there. We cannot change the economy overnight, but there are some very simple safeguards that we can put in place that will bring us economic relief.

Family Planning

When we consider the fact that 7 out of 10 Black children in America are born out of wedlock, it is easy to see why we remain in poverty. Unplanned children have a devastating effect on a family's finance. The repercussions are even direr in the case of single parent families. Most Black women are just a couple of paychecks away from being homeless. Sisters can choose to practice multiple forms of birth control so that in case one form fails, the other method can act as a safety net. Afrikan men can make the wise choice to wear condoms during every sexual experience as well. We are sickened by the weak excuses we hear from ignorant post-Pride men about the fallibility of condoms. Most men that claim that a condom failed during sexual activity *and* that a pregnancy resulted from that failure are bald-faced liars. That they are childish and stupid enough to think that anyone actually believes them only further nauseates us. The modern slave is a weakling by definition. The entire world is against him. It's the condom's fault that he has children that he can't support. It's the woman's fault for getting pregnant in the first place. The consequences of unplanned pregnancies go beyond mere financial irritations. A new child means less space in the home. Cramped conditions plus increased financial pressures is a recipe for high blood pressure. This may also cause the parent to subconsciously resent the new baby as he or she is seen as the direct cause of all the misery. Why do we continue to put ourselves through this torment? How is it that sisters have money to get their nails done every other week, but none for birth control? How is it that Black men have money for CDs, DVDs and marijuana, but they can't find three dollars for a box of condoms?

Those of us that are already in a situation where there are unplanned children and mounting expenses can still take advantage of this wisdom. If they are already stretched to the limit and stressed out, why add more children to the equation? Slaves dream about having a trouble-free life. Everybody does! The problem is that the slave's dream always involves someone else descending from the clouds and saving them. That has never happened in all of recorded history. No one has ever come along and solved all of the world's problems, leaving us in perfect peace and harmony. It's not going to happen now. No one is going to drive through the ghetto passing out money. Those that hold their breath in expectation of winning the lottery will surely suffocate. The only thing that will save us from a flood of unplanned (and even unwanted) pregnancies is action. There are Planned Parenthood and Free Clinic facilities in every major city in the United States. Additionally, there are several reliable online drugstores that will deliver birth control products right to our homes.

Savings

While 90% of Afrikan Americans have checking accounts, a very dismal percentage also has accounts set aside for savings. The most common excuse for failure to save money is, "I barely have enough money for my regular bills. How can I start saving?" Afrikan people must realize that priorities have a direct effect on our quality of life. If buying shoes and clothes is more important than paying our rent, we will be the best dressed homeless people in the shelters. If having every possible feature on one's cell phone- from text messaging to email to daily horoscope updates- is more important than dental care, then we are total fools. Anyone that has suffered from an abscessed tooth will attest to this. We must always ask ourselves if there is any place in our budget where we can put away at least ten dollars a month. As with family planning, action is the only thing that will improve our financial condition. Black people must open savings accounts and make regular deposits. This is an easy thing to do, especially for Afrikan Americans that routinely waste money on tooth-rotting candy, soda, and artery-clogging fast food. Our savings accounts will supplement our income during the lean times. Savings often make the difference between freezing and having heat in our homes. Black people also must teach our children to be savers. The best birthday gift that an Afrikan child can get is a savings account!

Education

Education is a long-term investment. It is for this reason that so few in the post-Pride contingent take advantage of higher learning. The childish slave mind cannot understand ventures that do not provide immediate dividends. The slave doesn't get any money for going to college. He fails to see that higher learning increases our financial opportunities. His tiny mind cannot grasp the concept that associating with upwardly mobile people increases our circle of business contacts. The tremendous gains in social status that degreed Afrikans enjoy are also of no consequence to the slave mind. Educated Afrikans have the power to make high-level decisions, to make inroads into the vast abyss of depression and other mental remnants of the ravages of slavery, to invent, to treat diseases and improve the quality of life for thousands. The modern slave is unimpressed. His vision of power involves degrading Black people. If a college is not going to teach him how to rustle up a herd of desperate Black and Caucasian women that will bend over and expose their genitalia for him and his friends, the school is worthless. If the Geometry teacher is not going to give him a brand new car after class, the teacher "ain't talking about shit". In fact, any person who is not emptying their pockets to please a modern slave is a "nobody". Anyone not providing money, the use of an automobile, or drugs to the post-Pride generation is worthless. This explains the rampant disrespect directed at parents and elders by today's modern slaves. Good advice is wasted on them. They don't hear anything their parents say unless they are being given money to buy gold teeth and other props to buttress their pathetic street image. Post-Pride teenagers bear exceptional malice towards their teachers. They believe that teachers are their enemies. Popular rap lyrics express this sentiment. Rappers tell us that they found the roach to riches the day they cursed out their teachers and quit school. Misguided Black teenagers thus come to believe that educators are somehow standing in the way of their prosperity. Education is impossible for the post-Pride slave because it requires some level of self-respect and common sense. If American universities were to offer courses on how to disrespect and murder Black people, rappers and R&B singers would graduate magna cum laude. It is the only thing that they truly love. Education is a fortress against hard times because it gives us more income. There is more left over to save and invest. Furthermore, education gives us the opportunity to travel, own our own homes, and open legitimate businesses.

Living Within Our Means

McDonald's and Burger King certainly had Afrikan Americans in mind when they installed debit/credit machines in their restaurants. Black people are notorious for using credit cards for nonessentials. Credit is appealing because it allows us to live in a fantasy world. We simply take the things we want, swipe our magic card, and go home to enjoy them without paying a single dime. A few weeks later, a gigantic credit card bill arrives in the mail. We pay not only for our purchases, but staggering amounts of interest and other fees. This is madness. If we couldn't afford the items *before* all of the interest and other charges were added, what do we imagine will happen when the statement comes? Whether we believe we will have the money to pay our credit card bills, Black people must realize that every single swipe of the credit card puts us into debt. We should only go into debt for essentials. Fast food is not an essential. New shoes are not essential for a person who already has a pair of shoes. With the current recession, many Americans are now forced to use credit cards for groceries and utility bills. Those of us that wasted our credit and put ourselves in debt for sunglasses, video games, and value meals have been reduced to borrowing from relatives and begging the gas company not to cut off their heat.

Our eyes can get us into a world of debt. The best way to control impulsive spending is by staying out of shops when we have no money in the first place. The mall is not a singles bar. It is a place of business. A mall is commerce, interest, and taxes. Many Afrikan Americans believe that they are spending quality time with their loved ones by taking them for a stroll through the mall. As soon as we are there, we become confused and blinded by all the great deals and flashy new gadgets. We ought to stay out of stores when our funds are low. We should avoid merchant-type websites as well. A little common sense goes a long way. None of us would dive into a pool that has no water in it. Yet we have no problem spending money that doesn't exist. The sad truth is that much of the wasted money in the Afrikan American community is funneled into slave activities. This childish, often unspoken competition between Black people will leave us all bankrupt. Trying to dress better than our neighbors and drive finer cars than our relatives are all desperate cries for attention. Those of us that have not lost our Afrikan minds feel sorry for today's coons that blast their music and put on a show as they drive down the street. We know that these cars will soon be repossessed or riddled with bullets. It is sobering when we see Black women and their children at bus stops, covered in jewelry and leather. We know that these children are struggling in math and that they've never read a book that wasn't assigned in class. The world knows that Black people can dress up on the outside. When are we going to do the right thing? When will we realize that we must first dress up our insides with self-respect and knowledge of self? Until we do, we will continue to make the same financial mistakes over and over. Our oppressors will continue to reap the benefits of our slave foolishness. Dance, Eshu! Dance!

CHAPTER SEVEN

The New Face of Willie Lynch

"Psychological and physical containment must be created for both [Blacks and horses]."
—From "Let's Make A Slave" By Willie Lynch as published by The Black Arcade Liberation Library; 1970

When we peel back the mask and peer through the fog of legend, we find the true face of "Willie Lynch". Beneath the mask, we find not a spineless klansman or some heartless Caucasian politician. Today, "Willie Lynch" is nothing more than the self-hating Negroes of hip hop and the slaves that support them. We have the power to liberate ourselves. Michelle Obama's ancestors toiled on the rice plantations of South Carolina. They endured unspeakable cruelties. But her love of education and sense of dignity has her and her beautiful daughters sleeping in the White House today. Would Obama have chosen her for a wife if she was covered in trashy tattoos, talking loud, or refusing to get an education? Eric Holder was born in the impoverished Bronx borough of New York and his intelligence and refusal to ever give up carried him all the way to his current position as the first Afrikan American Attorney General of the United States. Oprah Gail Winfrey was born to a low-income single mother in rural Mississippi, but look at her today! So who is the real Willie Lynch? Who tells little Black girls that they are destined to be whores, that they should "drop it like it's hot" instead of studying and getting a real job? Who tells our beautiful Afrikan boys that they are niggas? Who tells them to murder their own people? Who tells Black men that education and hard work is for suckers? No one, except the sniveling, genocidal fools of today's rap circuit.

Our Afrikan ancestors thought that they had found a friend in the Europeans. They could not have been more wrong! If we are ever to experience peace and dignity, we must learn, once and for all, how to tell the difference between an enemy and a friend. When we walk around, mindlessly repeating insipid rap lyrics and forcing our children to imitate their dress and mannerisms, we are sleeping with the enemy. After his election victory, one cowardly rapper remarked that "Obama would change the tone of hip hop." This is precisely what we would expect to hear from a weak, ignorant, slave-minded Sambo. Obama is not the one with the mic in his hand! Why should Obama change hip hop? The Sambos are the ones who are making the records. They are the ones spreading lies about our people. They are the ones selling crack and heroin, abandoning their children, and encouraging the murder of Black people on a daily basis. Is Obama responsible for that?

Hip hops so-called "artists" bear a hatred for Afrikan people that puts the cruelest slave owner to shame. They want every single one of us to suffer every day of our lives until we die. The icing on the cake would be death at their hands, in the throws of a drug overdose, or in an unmarked prison grave. We can hear the slaves arguing that *rappers don't hate Black people, they just love money!* This kind of "explanation" only convinces people who are stupid. Who doesn't love money? Oprah loves money! How many people has she poisoned with crack cocaine? Johnnie Cochran loved money, too. How many Black girls did he encourage to strip and behave like sexual beasts? The venerable Sas, Chief of the Bubi people of Bioko Island, West Afrika[39], loved money as well. Yet his people never kept slaves, nor did they ever sell a single soul to the Arabs or Europeans. In fact, the Bubis did not even have a word for "slave" in their language and had to borrow the term from the Europeans to describe the condition of the people around them who were being stolen from their coast. The one reading this book surely loves money as well. How many home invasions has the reader committed? How many drive-by shootings? Love of money does not mean that you encourage and participate in genocide. Hatred alone is what causes it.

Gangsta rappers tout the drug trade as a fast and easy way to make money. It is presented as an alternative to the eight-hour work day and the financial limitations of hourly wages. Afrikan people are wildly attracted to the gangsta mystique. We long for the wads of cash that the thug brandishes in his bejeweled fist. We covet the candy paint on the customized automobile that he drives down the street. Many Black women are intoxicated by all of the pretty, shiny things they possess. Like addicts, they will stoop to any and every level of obscenity just to have a few crumbs thrown their way. Gangsta rappers recognize this weakness of mind and principle. They get their sense of power from the fact that for a few dollars and a ride in their car, women will not only provide for their sexual needs, but those of all of their friends as well. It gives them a sense of pride to see grown Black men yapping at their heels like desperate puppies just for the chance to sit in their car and go to places that they go. They even find joy in the desperate acts of the fiends that buy their dope. Fancy toys, women, shopping sprees, and throngs of pathetic "jockers" (hangers-on) and dope

39   Formerly known as the Island of Fernando Po.

heads are only one side of thug life. In order to be a "thug" or to "move weight', a person must make several sacrifices and transformations. They must be willing to destroy lives. They can't make money unless someone is desperate and addicted to drugs. They must fight, shoot, and kill as well. As soon as one clique starts making money, other jealous gangs will try to come in and take over their territory. They must also degrade their families and our Black heritage. Afrikan people have never been purveyors of death. We were not the ones who pushed opium onto the Chinese. We did not peddle hashish throughout the Middle East, nor did we introduce the Native Americans to "fire water"[40].

Rappers brag about smoking marijuana, but crack cocaine is touted as the road to economic freedom in popular hip hop lyrics. So called because of the crackling sound that it makes as it is "cooked", crack cocaine is a highly addictive and toxic agent. Studies reveal that crack-addicted rats will choose the drug over food and water. Rats will also take incredibly painful electric shocks just to get another "hit". If they are left unsupervised, they will eat or inject crack voraciously until death. Crack addiction is easily recognizable. Smokers instantly lose interest in feeding themselves, resulting in a skeletal appearance that is indeed disturbing to observe. Their eyes acquire a glazed, desperate and slightly threatening affect. They often lack adequate body fat. Their cheek bones, shoulders, and knee caps press against their dry, ashy skin. Alternately, they are covered in sweat and look as if someone submerged them in a vat of baby oil. Sisters with beautiful figures and gorgeous hair become mummy look-alikes. Many bear a strong resemblance to the Crypt Keeper. People who

---

40   Distilled liquor.

smoke crack and snort or inject heroin begin to lose their hair. What remains on their head becomes wiry, dry, and wild. Crack-heads, as they are frequently dubbed throughout the Afrikan community, also lose all of their valuables through pawning or selling in order to obtain cash for further crack purchases. It is heartbreaking to watch a brother or sister slowly sell off all of their possessions just for another hit. Our sisters' necklaces, rings, and watches begin to disappear, piece by piece. Our brothers pawn their VCRs, DVD players, video game consoles, and television sets. Eventually, all of the high-price items are gone, and they resort to selling their furniture, appliances, and their clothes, often until they have only one outfit left. It is at that point that many dope fiends begin to steal, although we must point out that for those who never had any of the aforementioned possessions, the stealing begins immediately. Theft by means of burglary and armed robbery are somewhat common, but the most popular targets of the dope-head's sticky fingers are their own friends, relatives, and neighbors.

Living in Crack's Shadow

Black families are truly taken through the wringer when one of us is afflicted by chemical slavery. We take our relatives and spouses to hospitals for inpatient drug treatment programs. We write to them and visit them when they are in jail. But even the most patient families begin to see that only the addict can break their chemical chains, and ultimately many crack fiends end up on the streets. Dope fiends put our lives in jeopardy by bringing their crack-head friends into our homes. They lie endlessly to our faces. It is impossible to keep company with dope-heads because of their poor hygiene. Who wants to be around a woman who is covered in sickly-smelling sweat and who constantly scratches her matted, ratty hair? Afrikan women and men frequently perform sexual "favors" in exchange for dope. This is also another avenue of exposure to the HIV virus. Black men who are slave to the glass pipe or the needle are especially embarrassing. Their behavior is more revolting than that of female fiends. Like female addicts, they pawn, steal, and lie to their friends. They also dabble in the sex trade, performing oral sex on other men in exchange for drugs or money. They frequently smell of anus and armpits and are exceptionally prone to violence. Male dope fiends often prey upon the elderly and the poor in a particularly inhumane fashion.

Crack is a consummate destroyer of all aspects of life. In 2004, 70 percent of homicides in Greensboro and High Point, North Carolina were linked to crack cocaine. The effects of crack and heroin use span the gamut of physical maladies- disturbances in heart rhythm, heart attacks, respiratory failure, strokes, chest pain, and gastrointestinal complications[41]. People who inject cocaine are at increased risk for contracting HIV and other blood-borne diseases. The drug has literally devastated Afrikan life in places such as New Orleans, Detroit, Los Angeles, and St. Louis. Dope is also a major contributor to the emasculation of Afrikan men. Addiction means dependency. It is impossible for an addict to be his own man. He is a slave to the needle, the powder or the glass pipe. He is at the mercy of sadistic and heartless dope dealers. He is a primitive-minded nomad, wandering wherever the supply of crack and the degrading

41   National Institute on Drug Abuse: *Crack Cocaine*. March 2005.

stunts he pulls to obtain it takes him. Preying upon the elderly and the weak further warps his sense of manhood. These fiends learn that all they must do in order to get fast cash is push an old woman to the ground and snatch her purse. When the need for dope strikes them, they automatically begin to search for victims- young women walking to their cars in parking lots, old people out on their daily walks, trusting neighbors who leave their windows ajar. Such pathetic displays of weakness and stupidity often leave innocent people of all races hospitalized or in their graves. Crack addiction and manhood are exclusive characteristics. We can be one or the other, but not both.

The post-Pride stratagem against Black youth begins long before our teenage boys and girls are seduced (or forced) into the dope/gang deathstyle. While we dance to slave music and worship rappers, Black fetuses suffer strokes and heart attacks in the womb as a result of exposure to dope. Crack-exposed babies are more likely to be born weighing less than 5 ½ pounds. Underweight babies are 20 times more likely to die in their first month of life than normal-weight babies. Many are also sentenced to life-long disabilities such as cerebral palsy and mental retardation. Cocaine-exposed babies also tend to be born with smaller heads, which generally reflect smaller brains. A 2002 study at Case Western Reserve University found that cocaine-exposed 2-year olds were twice as likely as unexposed children to have significant delays in mental development. Rappers are extremely knowledgeable about the goings-on in the "hood". They know about the malformed Black babies, the 9-year old girl who still wears diapers and the 3-year old boy who cannot stop screaming and crying. Yet they continuously praise this infanticide and the masses of unconscious Black people continue to groove along.

Dope-slinging crushes Black children and grinds Afrikan families into dust. Our babies watch in terror and confusion as the furniture in their homes disappears, food becomes scarce, and their parents become increasingly irrational and often violent. Their beautiful, sad brown eyes take in the drug game on a daily basis. Black babies see their mothers prostituting themselves. They witness their mothers being severely beaten by pimps or by other crack-heads in disputes over dope and money. They are utterly defenseless against the endless parade of derelicts that their drug-crazed mothers and/or fathers allow into the home. We all read with horror the tragic story of little Erica Michelle Green, the 4 year-old Afrikan girl whose PCP abusing father kicked to death, then beheaded and disposed of like garbage with the help of her own mother (2001). An appalling number of Black babies are also at risk for molestation due to drug trafficking in their homes and neighborhoods. Many even become infected with gonorrhea or other venereal diseases in the process. Our children often find themselves at the mercy and whim of the racist and largely ineffective Child Protective Services. This is an agency known for taking legal control over Black children and then "losing" them, as reports from several states (Florida being chief among them) have shown. According to New York City's Human Resources Administration, reports of drug-related child abuse surged by 72 percent in a single year following the influx of crack. The number of cases of abuse and neglect filed in the Family Court has increased almost six-fold since 1984. They are shuffled from one foster home to the next. It is not surprising that many exhibit antisocial behavior at very young ages. They are left to fend for themselves, often joining or forming gangs for protection. The gang will support itself via dope sales or theft. The cycle continues. When we cruise up and down the city streets blasting music that celebrates slinging dope, we are admitting that we find the destruction of Black childhood entertaining. We are also celebrating the imprisonment of Afrikan potential. Modern slave rappers make frequent references to "having them little niggas slinging rocks" or "posted up" with automatic weapons. These gold-toothed clowns are actually proud of having blocked the path of young Black girls and boys who might have become engineers, educators, and doctors. They find it "cute" that they have steered our babies onto a road that leads only to prison or early graves. They love the fact that they have turned Black neighborhoods into corridors of death. It is not enough to merely take rap- an Afrikan tool of liberation- and use it to degrade all things Afrikan. The post-Pride mentality is not satisfied with the mere erosion of our beautiful musical heritage. Its aim is the wholesale obliteration of Afrikan people; to wipe us from the face of the Earth. That's how much your favorite gangsta rapper loves us.

Thug Dreams

When the brutality of the dope game is presented in rap lyrics, it is a joke couched within some play on words that colorfully describes the nigga's head being blown apart and mocks the weeping of the deceased's mother. Mainstream rap music functions as the dreamscape of the post-Pride imagination. The filth that spews from their jewel-encrusted slave mouths represents their deepest desires and wildest dreams. It amounts to a wholesale rejection of Afrikan heritage. We have been famed poets since the days of the griot. Brothers no longer weave their words into breathtaking tapestries that carry the listener into fancies of love, sorrow, hope, and strength. Today it is vivid depictions of blood and wailing mothers. It is what they want and what they like. This comes as no surprise when we consider the source. We quite correctly anticipate violence and ignorance from thugs and drug dealers. But what sort of people would not only support these genocidal ramblings, but embrace them as part of their culture? The truth is that many of us have become distracted. We are too busy being followers and salivating over the diamonds and platinum chains. The waves of blood that drench our neighborhoods are difficult to ignore, so the clowns of the music industry bring out more toys, cars, mansions, and guns to keep our minds off of what is happening to our people. This is what happens when we let ourselves be put to sleep. We behave like children. It is easy to distract a child. Pediatricians use puppets and stuffed animals to distract children from the syringe in their other hand. Black people need to stop looking at what rappers have and start paying attention to what they say.

Sambo Thinks He's Smart

The post-Pride element congratulates itself for their superior intellect and invulnerability. Gangsta rappers continuously remind us that they are "too smart" to be caught up in drug busts. They tell us that they are perpetually armed and therefore untouchable. These lyrics reveal the flaws in the post-Pride stratagem. Rappers are obviously not untouchable. Several rappers who claimed to be so are now resting in their graves. Others have been shot or locked away in prison. They are not nearly as intelligent as they tend to believe. It does not take intelligence to be a slave. In fact, the opposite is true.

Afrikans were barred from learning to read and write because gaining knowledge made us *less likely* to settle for being slaves. They claim to be fearless, but as soon as they are in the police's clutches, they instantly tell everything they know in order to get a lighter sentence. What they don't know, they simply ad lib. But we were brought here to hand one another over to Massa. If not in handcuffs, then modern slaves are content to hand over bullet ridden or drug-overdosed corpses. Either way is fine with them. They are just being good slaves. Rappers portray drug dealers as powerful people, but what "powers" do they possess? They can purchase large homes and get gadgets and toys. They have the ability to rip families apart, to deprive children of their mothers and fathers. They have the capacity to engage in terrifying home invasions and turn one innocent family's evening into a multiple wake.

Poverty is a form of bondage. It traps its victims in underdeveloped, often dangerous neighborhoods and bars access to any means of improving their lives, such as education and medical treatment. Ignorance is a form of slavery because it traps its victims in an extremely narrow mindset that likewise bars access to means of improving one's life. Drug addiction is also bondage, and our choice to glorify the dope game and its hollow, violent rhetoric is a foolish one indeed. The slave trade was not simply about the displacement of 100 million Afrikan men and women. It was about the transfer of power. Ever since the moment that we began to allow our culture to be shaped by ignorant yet charismatic Black spin doctors, we have been without the blessings, benefits, and protection that come with being a free people. Initially, a few Afrikans must certainly have found it cute and funny to sell other Afrikans to the Europeans. But the cuteness soon faded when the Continent fell into disarray, violence, and famine and the sellers found themselves in chains on ships headed for the Americas. Our power and control over the Continent was lost. Dope likewise transfers the addict's life in to the hands of dope pushers and the government. Both the crack addict and the pusher eventually come under the control of various government agencies. They are both locked up, observed, controlled. Black children find themselves under the government's control as well. They are taken to foster homes that are sometimes worse than their real homes. Their every move is dictated by the courts. This is the reason why it is imperative that Black people learn our history. Our story is not a useless list of facts and dates, nor is it a collection of stories about people and places that have absolutely no relation to our present condition. It helps us to recognize patterns and trends so that we can avoid repeating the mistakes of the past. Our failure to learn from our history has come with a high price. Five centuries after the cuteness wore off, we remain poor and disenfranchised whether we live in Morant Bay, Bamako, or Boston.

It is well known that Black people have neither the resources nor the freedom of movement required to set up and maintain the multi-national network of runners, distributors, and suppliers that exists today. It is when we ask the question of how crack magically appeared in our neighborhoods that the puppet strings on Black dope dealers truly begin to show. Congresswoman Maxine Waters conducted an extensive and multi-national investigation into the subject. On March 16, 1998, Congresswoman Waters testified before the House Permanent Select Committee on Intelligence that, in order to "fund its Contra war activities...the CIA directed this drug trafficking operation out of two hangers, using the Contra supply network as the route for shipping drugs into the U.S." She revealed that the dope was first made available for sale in Los Angeles and New Orleans, and that "U.S. State Department funds, authorized by Congress for humanitarian assistance, was paid to drug traffickers. In some cases, these drug traffickers received the State Department funds *after having been indicted by federal law enforcement agencies on drug charges and, in other cases, were the subject of pending investigations by those agencies* (emphasis ours)". Thus, we ultimately find that the thugs who claim to be "breaking tha law" and "duckin' them people" are actually operating *inside* the law, serving as agents in the destruction of their own people. And like the foolish West Afrikans who participated in the beginnings of the slave trade, these saggy drawers wearing killers suffer the same fate as their victims. They are either murdered at some point or they end up as legal slaves, serving incredibly long sentences on legal plantations.

Rappers are pathological liars when it comes to describing Afrikan people. They associate dope with our race, but Black people are neither the source nor are we the major consumers of drugs in America. Afrikans in the United States account for less than 25% of the country's drug abusers. The Substance Abuse and Mental Health Services Administration's 1998 Summary Report revealed that "most current illicit drug users are white. There were an estimated 9.9 million whites (72 percent of all users), 2.0 million blacks (15 percent), and 1.4 million Hispanics (10 percent) who were current illicit drug users in 1998"[42]. Afrikans, however, make up 38.6% of those arrested for drug violations and more than 42% of those in federal prisons for drug offenses. 58% of all Americans

---

42   Substance Abuse and Mental Health Services Administration. National Household Survey on Drug Abuse: Summary Report 1998.

serving time in state institutions for drug felonies happen to be Afrikans. According to Paige M. Harrison and Allen J. Beck's 2004 report entitled *Prison and Jail Inmates at Midyear 2004*, "When total incarceration rates are estimated separately by age group, black males in their twenties and thirties are found to have high rates relative to other groups. Among the more than 2.1 million offenders incarcerated on June 30, an estimated 576,600 were black males between ages 20 and 39. Among males age 25–29, 12.6% of blacks were in prison or jail compared to 3.6% Hispanics and 1.7% of whites...Although incarceration rates drop with age, the percentage of black males age 45–54 in prison or jail in 2004 was an estimated 4.5%. [That was] more than twice the highest rate (1.7%) among white males (age 30–34)".

George Goldman, an economist from the University of California at Berkeley, directed the first comprehensive study of the economic impact of the California Prison Authority. Released in 1998, his report showed that California prison factories and farms are responsible for over $150 million in direct sales on an annual basis. Prison work programs in California are voluntary. Inmates upholster furniture, make license plates, eyeglass lenses and jeans. The pay scale ranges from 30–95 cents per hour. In California, only government agencies are permitted to purchase prison products, but in Nevada and Oregon, convicts make automobiles and jeans for retail sale. In 1997, Oregon's jeans (called "Prison Blues") were so popular that prison factories were unable keep up with the demand. According to Lucia Hwang's 1998 report *Working for Nothing: The Failure of Prison Industry Programs*, then-governor Pete Wilson planned to use the Prison Industry Authority to "make the prisons pay for themselves". This left more money for salaries and employment perks for the prison bureaucracy. Unfortunately, it is not until after years in prison that many brothers realize that they were nothing more than the punch line in a long and cruel joke.

Afrikans in the 1950's met with tremendous violence simply for exercising their right to vote. Nothing stands in our way today except the Sambos of the rap world and the mindset that they promote. 13 percent of all adult Afrikan men in the United States (1.4 million) are disenfranchised, representing one third of the total disenfranchised population and reflecting a rate of 7 times the national disenfranchisement average. Though 4.6 million Afrikan men voted in 1996, 1.4 million were unable to vote due to their criminal or post-conviction status[43]. These are votes that could have been used to empower the Afrikan community. These votes might have back politicians who would have made improvements in our schools and brought opportunities to our people. As we blast post-Pride hip pop that glorifies any part of the dope game - the violence, the money, or the schemes involved- we must ask ourselves whether or not those Afrikan and Caucasian people who were lynched and tortured for attempting to register Black voters died in vain. We cannot help but wonder if Andrew Goodman, Michael Schwerner, and James Cheney were murdered viciously in 1964 so that we could celebrate putting ourselves in a position where we are unable to vote.

We cannot overlook the impact that criminal convictions will have on future conscious movements. Parole officers can use their powers as means of controlling free-thinking brothers and sisters, calling them in for drug tests and pestering them with searches just to scare off their free-thinking friends. One

---

43   Fellner, Jamie and Mauer, Marc; *Losing the Vote: The Impact of Felony Disenfranchisement Laws in the United States.*

in three Afrikan men between the ages of 20 and 29 years old is under correctional supervision or control[44]. Our sisters find themselves in a similar situation. Of all Black women, sisters aged 35–39 have the highest rate of incarceration- 993 per 100,000. This rate is more than 5 times that of white females in this age group. It is foreseeable that probation and parole status will be used as a weapon against future Afrikan luminaries.

Getting Free

Our situation is a challenging one, but we are a people who weave difficulties into beautiful patterns, unforgettable expressions, and exquisite melodies. Every day, more and more Afrikans are breaking the chains of ignorance and drug abuse. Many return to the community armed with wisdom gained from their painful experiences. They reach back to help those of us who are still struggling. In England, BUBIC (Bringing Unity Back Into the Community) won a Peace Award for their project, which uses former crack addicts to get Afrikan people off of dope. By 2005, BUBIC had 16 ex-crack users walking the streets all day, talking to users and encouraging them to come and join one of their support groups. The founder, Larry Babalola, described the program as a "project [that] exists to help any addicts, but we target people from the Black community because, at present, Black users are poorly represented within the traditional treatment service." In 2000, Rene Stockton of Harlem, New York graduated with honors from Hunter College. Just a few years before, crack addition

---

44   Mauer, M & Huling, T.; *Young Black Americans and the Criminal Justice System: Five Years Later.*

had the brother living in his car and eating from garbage cans on the Upper East Side. Today, he works as a Social Services Supervisor, offering strength to other brothers and sisters who are victims of the dope game. Another example is our sister Giovanni Jackson, who was reduced by crack addiction to sleeping in doorways at night. But in 2005, after delivering herself from the demons of dependency, she returned to shelters in California and donated 100 care packages to people who were still trying to rid themselves of the habit. This and other such gestures show those of us who want to change that there is hope.

Many former gang bangers, thugs, and dope dealers have also given up their destructive ways. They return to the community to help our people take back our minds. Some become successful and lead by quiet example and others go out in the streets and confront our drug and gang problems in the trenches. Actor Charles Dutton took control of his life after violence caused him to spend more than seven years in prison. He graduated from college and began to study theatre. He was later accepted into the Yale School of Drama and has had an exemplary acting career, both on stage and the silver screen. Reverend Leon Kelly takes a proactive approach, using gruesome videos of prison violence and autopsies to show young people the true face of gang life. In Los Angeles, former gang member Bo Taylor founded a street ministry called Unity One which offers employment to young people who have been released from prison. He also works with incarcerated gang members, teaching them the social skills needed to interact with people of different races and gang affiliations. He has worked with more than 1,900 inmates. Every day, brothers and sisters are choosing life over death. We choose strength over weakness and growth instead of destruction. Every day, a brother or sister listens carefully to the messages spewing from his or her speakers and begins to wonder why we celebrate that which degrades us. Our community is given a boost whenever a young brother or sister turns away from the deathstyle and truly begins to live. We are in need of their strength, their boldness, and their quick wits. Our community is given a boost whenever a young brother or sister turns away from the deathstyle and truly begins to live.

Black people realize the enormity of the drug situation in our communities. We are beginning to see thug rappers and their drug-endorsing messages for what they are. The momentum is building. Afrikans everywhere are starting to reject the insanity of drug rap. But it is not enough to simply say that "they" don't represent us. We must make it clear that we have no use for "music" that praises selling dope and going to prison. Afrikan people must boycott radio stations that play this garbage. The DJs of these stations are likely non-Blacks who are exploiting our culture or slaves who ought to be out of work. The same is true of video channels and award ceremonies that promote genocide in our community. Black children must not be allowed to listen to it in our presence, nor should we prepare them for gang life at home. Black parents are doing nothing but grooming their children for penitentiary time. We buy them music that details how to "cook" or manufacture drugs, how to divide it up, and how to shoot up the neighborhood in order to protect the dope. We then dress them in gangsta apparel. They are all ready for the modern plantation.

The post-Pride contingent expends a great deal of energy seeking out ways to destroy their lives. They skip school to be with the gang and then spend their lives ducking the police or each other. They are beaten, arrested, robbed, and humiliated.

Dope fiends and their dealers could put the same energy into rescuing themselves. Addicts have plenty of time to sell their bodies and steal from their relatives. They could spend the same time visiting churches, mosques, and social service offices until they find some help. Drug dealers have ample time to lurk in the streets passing out poison. They apparently have 15 or 20 years to waste in prison being molested by other men. They could choose to use their energy seeking out mentors. All of the excuses that they might offer for not getting help are stale ones. That expired years ago with the creation of the Internet. We must learn to use the computer for more than viewing pornography and downloading slave music. The ignorance of the post-Pride era squanders the lessons of the past and sentences our people to several hundred more years of second-class citizenship. The instruments of choice- flashy jewels, sex, shiny automobiles, and cash- are merely weapons of mass distraction intended to bedazzle and mislead us into dancing into our graves.

CHAPTER EIGHT

Wade In The Water

"A little rain each day will fill the rivers to overflowing."
—Liberian proverb

The morning's silence was broken many times that day. The birds twittered and rustled as they congregated in the trees. Roosters shouted in awe of the magenta, orange, and pink streaks that announced the rising sun. The horn blew, followed by the whisper of shuffling feet. The procession of slaves on Mr. Sanders' plantation was as orderly as a line of marching soldiers. They held hoes, sacks, shovels, and empty buckets instead of rifles. None of them spoke. They lined up quietly in front of the slave quarters and headed for the cotton fields.

Katie Rowe didn't think about time when she was in the fields. It was best to just keep working. Keep working. She sang to keep her mind off of the fierce Oklahoma sun as it sailed higher in the sky. An hour passed. The horn blew. The slaves stopped singing. They looked at one another. But they didn't stop working. Their black and brown hands moved with a surgeon's precision. Minutes passed. Katie went back to singing her song. A couple of slaves on the other side of the field picked up her song and sang it back. They added a few lines of their own. The horn blew. The crew leader looked across the field at the Big House. The porch was empty. *Ain't time to go in yet*, one young man observed. *Dat our horn,* the crew leader remarked, shaking the dirt loose from his hoe. He slung it over his shoulder and headed for the Big House. *We betta go on in.* The slaves were confused. If they ignored the horn and continued to work, they might be beaten, killed, or sold away from their families. They might also lose their pitiful food rations for a week. If they left their work in the fields to go see what was happening at the Big House, they could be beaten, hanged, or sold away for being lazy. Some of them lagged behind. They watched the tall, thin crew leader's torn shirt blowing in the spring breeze as he turned the bend that led to the courtyard.

Master Sanders was not there. In his place was a tall Caucasian man dressed in a Yankee officer's uniform. He had white hair and a long, snowy beard. He looked over the group of slaves, squinting as if trying to find something he'd lost. *Is everybody here?* The officer asked. The crew leader turned to the rest of the group. He knew that all of the slaves were present, but pretended to count them anyway. Doing otherwise might have incurred the white man's rage. *Yessuh. We all here.* The officer changed the subject. *Do you know today's date?* he asked. *No suh. We don't know,* the crew leader answered honestly. *Well, I want you to remember this date, because you will always remember this day,* the officer began. *Today is June the 4th, in the year eighteen hundred and sixty-five. Today you are free. You don't have to go by the horn anymore. I want you to understand this. You are your own boss. You have all the same rights as me, or Mr. Sanders, or any other white person. May the Lord bless you.* He then climbed atop his horse and rode towards town. They never saw him again.

All of the Afrikans were motionless until distance swallowed the silhouette of the Yankee on his horse. Some of the women cried. Everyone prayed, but only for a few moments. The plantation then became a beehive of activity. They ran to their shacks and gathered their pots and pans in sacks that they made from their bedding. Some of them tied the ends of their bed sheets to sturdy sticks and slung them over their backs. It took only a few minutes for them to gather what few belongings they had. Soon they were all back in the courtyard again. It was then that the question that had been brewing in all of their minds began to possess them. Katie thought it. All of them thought it. When they were furiously packing their things, they were able to ignore it. Now there was nothing left to do. The crew leader had no experience at being a free man. He fell into the role that slavery assigned him. He was used to being the first one to speak. Indeed, he was accustomed to having to speak for the entire group of slaves. He let the question fall from his generous Afrikan lips: *Where we gon' go*[45]*?*

It would please us immensely if we could stand before that crew leader today. We could tell him in vivid detail about where he and all of the other emancipated slaves would eventually go. We would tell him that some of the newly freed Afrikans headed for Kansas. They rolled up their sleeves and built an entire township. It is erroneous to believe that the slaves were helpless people. Our ancestors were the reason that there were crops in the fields. They were the ones that tanned the leather. They were the blacksmiths and the carpenters. Slaves also tended the animals. It was perfectly natural for them to plan, build, and run entire cities. They had done it for others in the past without being paid a red cent. Now they were doing it for themselves. Nicodemus was founded in 1877. Several drawings and photographs of the town are accessible today. The most impressive features in the town were the

---

45   Adapted from *The Slave Narratives Volume 13.*

hotels and the church. It was a Baptist Church. Jenny Smith
Fletcher was the wife of its founder. She was also one of the first
charter members of the African Methodist Episcopal Church.
Nicodemus offered jobs, land, and education to Black people
from all over the country. In 1886, former slaves built the town
of Eatonville, Florida. Eatonville was an orderly town with
abundant commerce and solid family values. Residents enjoyed
an array of services including a reliable post office and a well-
stocked general store. But these Black towns offered much more
than creature comforts. Reconstruction Era Afrikan American
towns gave our ancestors the opportunity to heal at last. They
were officially free no matter where they went. But there were
several compelling reasons why they should not remain in the
towns where they had been enslaved. Continuing to live in
close quarters with those that had raped them, molested their
children, and destroyed their families would only keep those
abuses fresh in their minds. There was also a high probability of
violence. White Americans were angry about all of the death
and pain that the Civil War had brought to their families. In
their rage, it was easier to claim that the liberation of Black
people had cost them everything than to acknowledge the
truth[46]. Many ex-slaves fled their home towns in fear of blind
retribution. Black townships offered relief from fear. These
were places where we could walk the streets at any hour of the
day or night without being stopped, questioned, or assaulted.
These were places where we could visit the depths of tenderness.
We could meet, fall in love, and marry without asking anyone's

---

46   The Civil War was fought to prevent the Southern states
from forming their own country. The Northern states would have
lost the vast revenue and taxes garnered by the South's booming agricultural enterprises. Afrikan Americans were promised freedom
if we fought for the North only after it became clear that the North
could not win the war without us.

permission. Black people in Eatonville could enjoy the natural bond between mother and child, sister and brother, and husband and wife without fear of being sold away from one another. These Afrikan American cities were places where we could be ourselves and enjoy the fruits of our labor at last. And we could sing! We could raise our voices to the heavens. Not to distract ourselves from the painful, stifling sun. Not in protest to horrendous mistreatment. We could finally sing from a place of pure joy. If Uncle Crew Leader were here today, we could tell him that when our people left the plantations, they proved themselves to be resourceful and capable. There were roughly 100 Afrikan American towns in the United States. Their residents were self-reliant. We dispensed justice. We solved our own problems. Communalism ruled the day. With our bare hands, we created havens of opportunity, love, and trust.

Mr. Sanders was staunchly opposed to educating his slaves. For this reason, we are happy to answer Uncle Crew Leader's question, *Where we gon' go?* by telling him that we went to school. In 1875, the city of Normal, Alabama became home to the Alabama Agricultural and Mechanical University (AAME). The school was built by free Black people for all Black people. William Hooper Councill was its first President. He was also a former slave. Today, the descendants of slaves walk the halls of the University. AAME continues to provide quality education in the medical and botanical sciences. Ex-slaves in Nashville, Tennessee founded Meharry Medical College in 1876. They were helped by generous donations from the Methodist Episcopal Church. Today, students at this prestigious University conduct research in fluorescence activated cell sorting[47]. Langston

---

47   FACS is a process whereby groups of cells are analyzed according to their physical and chemical characteristics.

University was built in 1897 in Oklahoma, the home state of our Uncle Crew Leader. Long before there was a suffragist movement in America, Langston University endeavored to close the gender gap in higher education by recruiting Black women. The school still thrives today. Its doors are open to students of all races. There were more than one hundred and fifty Afrikan American colleges and universities. Many are still in operation. Morehouse College in Atlanta and Howard University in Washington, DC are two well known examples.

Very few slaves were permitted to indulge in sports. Our Uncle Crew Leader would be proud to know that when we left the plantations, we went on to become some of the world's most formidable athletes. He would be thrilled to know that Jackie Robinson[48] was the first person of any race to win the Major League Baseball Rookie of the Year Award in 1947. He also was the first Afrikan American to play for the Brooklyn Dodgers. Fifty years after his career began, Major League Baseball retired jersey number 42 (Robinson's number) so that no future player may use it. Arthur Ashe became the first Afrikan American to play on the United States Davis Cup team in 1963. In 1968, South Afrika's apartheid regime refused to grant him entry into the country based on the color of his skin. Ashe's response was a call for South Afrika's expulsion from the tennis circuit. It was unusual at the time. Tennis would not become associated with Black people until many decades later. Arthur Ashe remains the only Afrikan man ever to hold a title at Wimbledon or the Australian Open. Although his name is forever associated with baseball, Jackie Robinson was one of the founders of the Freedom National Bank. This was a financial institution owned and operated by Afrikan Americans in the 1960's. We would

---

48   Jack Roosevelt Robinson, 1919–1972.

fill several volumes were we to attempt to chronicle the many amazing feats accomplished by Afrikan Americans in sports. Bill Russell became the first Afrikan American head coach in the National Basketball Association in 1968. He went on to lead the Boston Celtics to two consecutive championship titles. We are indeed proud of our athletes. We are proud of Althea Gibson, Muhammad Ali, Michael Jordan, Venus Williams, April Holmes, Kevin Garnett, Lisa Leslie, Serena Williams, and Rickey Henderson who still holds the distinction of being one of baseball's most successful leadoff hitters.

Where did the descendants of the emancipated slaves go? Some went north, to places like New York City and Boston. We worked for the sanitation departments. We shoveled snow and manicured the lawns in front of municipal buildings. We donned ties and dresses and flocked into the office buildings. In Philadelphia, our sisters hovered over telephones and computer screens all day. When the days got long, they listened to Rose Royce's *Car Wash*. They listened to Midnight Star's *No Parking on the Dance Floor*. It made the hours pass quickly. Afrikans continued to survive the drama of the workplace by ritualizing the process in a way that is familiar to us all. Some of us migrated to the Midwest, to Detroit and Cleveland. Our uncles worked for the transit authority. They maintained the machines, collected tickets, assisted passengers, and mopped floors to the sounds of the Emotions singing *Best of My Love* and the Gap Band's *Burn Rubber*. We ran assembly lines at the Ford factory. Our mothers pulled double shifts at General Electric and General Motors while listening to Tom Browne's *Jamaica Funk* and One Way's *Cutie Pie*. Our fathers worked for Firestone and Goodyear. Their chests swelled with pride because the level of compensation for these jobs allowed them to provide for the family. Not just the basics. They were able to hire tutors to teach their daughters to play the violin. Their sons could go to baseball and football camps. After Christmas dinner in St. Louis, they turned up the radio and danced to Earth Wind & Fire's *September*. The ex-slaves and their progeny traveled west. Our cousins found work at the post office. They sorted mail and operated complex machinery. They worked split shifts. A Taste of Honey's *Sukiyaki* played softly in the background as they laughed and joked with their co-workers in the break room. In cities such as Oakland, Watts, and Portland, they danced the latest dances to Zapp & Roger's *More Bounce to the Ounce* and Cameo's *Candy*. Many of the former slaves and their offspring remained in the South. Our brothers joined the military. They went to Korea, Germany, England, and the Philippines. Whodini's *Five Minutes of Funk* and The Pointer Sisters' *Neutron Dance* blasting at the local bars reminded them of home. Our sisters filed into the universities. They became teachers, correcting papers late into the evening with Patti Labelle's *Love, Need & Want You* on the radio. They worked as nurses and spent many years lifting and turning patients. They worked in convalescent homes and were the only human contact that thousands of elderly men and women had during the final stage of their lives. Our aunties changed bedding, dispensed medication, or simply sat and talked with lonely and forgotten veterans and grandparents. Sometimes they just sat and listened to music. Sometimes they sang along with Stevie Wonder and his *Ribbons in the Sky*. It did not matter where we went. Black music was there for us every step of the way. Then something quite beautiful and possibly magical happened.

As our music spread around the world, it became the very language of life itself. Thus, a Caucasian woman in Georgia marks the end of a romantic relationship by playing Gloria

Gaynor's *I Will Survive* and Toni Braxton's *Love Should Have Brought You Home Last Night*. A Chinese man in New York blows off steam after a trying day on the job by blasting Kool Keith's *Get Off My Elevator*. A Nigerian man plays Luther Vandross' *So Amazing*, Howard Hewett's *For the Lover in You*, or even TLC's *Red Light Special* to create a romantic atmosphere. In the Philippines, prison inmates perform the zombie dance from Michael Jackson's *Thriller* video regularly as a form of therapy. We all fall in love to Heatwave's *Always and Forever*. We dance at weddings to Whitney Houston and Kool & the Gang. People all over the world learned that the emotions are universal. We were no longer frightened, downtrodden beasts. We taught them that we were human beings with aspirations, morals, and love in our hearts. Over time, many thousands of Caucasian people that had been victims of a racist upbringing came to see the error of their parents' ways. Whether we sing or rap, the world is listening. This is the true meaning of 'call and response'. Every singing or rapping Black man or woman is sending out a call. Afrikan music prompts us to act, even if our reaction is a simple bobbing of the head. It summons our emotions. The music calls us. We respond. Now it is easier to answer Uncle Crew Leader's question. Where did our people go? We went where our music took us.

No matter where we live, Afrikans find ourselves in a place that is strikingly similar to that of those on Mr. Sander's plantation. Emancipated slaves faced an economy that had been demolished by the Civil War. We presently suffer due to a financial crisis brought on in large part by fighting two wars at once. The Afrikans of 1865 were heading into the unknown. The world around them was literally changing overnight. There was so much for them to learn and many circumstances to which they had to adapt. Today, our world is threatened by global warming, shadowy terrorist organizations, violence, and disease. Every few months, a new gadget becomes a vital part of our lives. We too are finding that we must grow and change along with the world if we are ever to experience any measure of genuine happiness. Like our ancestors, we must ask ourselves, *where will we go?* We know exactly where we will go if we continue to follow today's minstrel show on its worldwide tour of ignorance. But where will we go if we escape from modern slavery? If we separate ourselves from the disgraceful thoughts and habits of those clapped in the irons of self-hatred?

The Rebirth of Communalism

In Post-pride videos and films, a large group of Black people in one place always means a party, a dope deal, or a robbery. Rarely are we cast as upwardly mobile citizens that congregate to produce something positive. Afrikans continue to debunk this myth. Every day, Black people from all over the world with progressive agendas are finding like-minded brothers and sisters. We are forming networks that bring jobs, information, and sanity back to our communities. Conscious Afrikans come from all walks of life. We are teachers, students, blue collar workers, businessmen, and entertainers. In the United States, the Hip Hop Summit Action Network (HSAN) uses the cultural relevance of rap music to "serve as a catalyst for education advocacy and other societal concerns fundamental to the well-being of at-risk youth". Their work goes beyond simply sitting at a table and talking. In conjunction with the Alliance for Quality Education, they mobilized over 100,000 New York City Public School students in a massive rally that pressured Mayor Michael R. Bloomberg into restoring $300 million in proposed cuts to the district's budget. The HSAN has also worked closely with the Recording Industry Association of America in support of the parental advisory program. This helps parents to monitor their children's music selection so that they can screen out inappropriate material. The HSAN also launched a public awareness campaign to protest the unfairness of the Rockefeller Drug Laws in New York. Their rally was attended by more than 70,000 people. This is a break with the selfish and destructive mentality that gangsta rap promotes. It proves that even the artists themselves understand that hip hop culture has drifted far off course. The forward momentum in the Black community knows no borders. Afrikans from every part of the world are reaching out to one another. It is a relief to know that when one Black hand reaches out, another Black hand is extended in friendship and brotherhood. For years, Carnaval dancers were the only representations of Afrikan heritage in the country of Uruguay. The past 15 years have seen a major shift in the interests of Afro-Uruguayans. There has been a significant increase in the creation of institutions dedicated to the study and preservation of Afrikan culture. The group Afro Mundo has even reached out to Afrikans in the United States, organizing scholastic conferences that focus on the Afrikan influences in South American art and culture.

Black organizations in the US have reached out to Continental Afrikans as well. The Oklahoma Black Chamber of Commerce launched the Oklahoma-Africa Trade and Investment Tour in 2006. This conference brought together government officials, entrepreneurs, investors, and bankers. The objective was not to ask for charity or to bemoan the condition of Afrikan people, but to find solutions that benefit our people at home and in the West. Most Afrikan countries are rich in natural resources. They are also home to plenty of educated citizens who are capable of putting together successful firms. In the West, we suffer from a scarcity of affordable production materials. Business connections between Continental and Diaspora Afrikans are beneficial to both parties. The two main goals of the Investment Tour were 1) to show how profitable investing in and trading with Afrikan countries can be and 2) promoting stronger relationships between the Continental and Diasporabased business communities. They also plan to serve as a hub for information on potential investment and trade opportunities in both Afrika and the United States. The tour represented a wide variety of business sectors: agriculture, oil production, health care, pharmaceuticals, mining, infrastructure, and even the packing and storage industries. While we do not have the resources to set up worldwide dope rings, we certainly are capable of collaborating with our cousins for the benefit of Black people on both sides of the Atlantic.

Money will not solve all of our problems. Today's slaves have millions of dollars at their disposal and all they have done is make things worse. Money is worthless in a slave's hands. All it can do is buy more destructive toys and provide a larger platform for the dissemination of nonsense. We cannot rescue ourselves through economic development alone. Addressing our social crises is of equal importance. Chief among our concerns is the immensely damaging misrepresentation of Black women in popular culture. Sexploitation rap has taken over as the prime venue for the assassination of the Black woman's character. But Black people are not afraid to speak up for our sisters. In 2004, when a misguided rapper swiped a credit card down the center of a sister's backside in one of his videos, the sisters at Spellman College refused to allow him to perform there. The ladies of the historically Black campus merely expressed what those of us who have not lost our minds have felt for years. We will speak up for our women. They sent a message of solidarity to our women all over the world. There are many such examples of our break with the manufactured identity. In 2002, the Muslim Student Association of Sarah Lawrence College in New York held a rally to protest the humiliating portrayal of women in mainstream rap and other avenues of popular culture. The rally was attended by Jurassic 5's Akil, spoken word artist Meqqa, and former Def Jam President Carmen Asshurst-Woodard. Members of the Afrikan, Latino, and Asian communities gathered for a dialogue about ways to minimize the effects of this rap insanity. A slave's first objective is to prove his loyalty to his master. He makes it abundantly clear that what happens to other Black people is not his problem. *Fuck dem niggas, Massa!* Showing concern for other Black people would imply a belief that Black people deserve empathy. While some rappers may care little or nothing for our women, Afrikans show time and time again that the rest of us do.

Black people in the Diasporas and Continental Afrika are all victims of the Western Holocaust, struggling to maintain our dignity and gain a foothold in the modern world. Continental Afrikans were also force-fed racist notions about Black inferiority for centuries. Like Black people in the West, they must choose between the manufactured identity and being their Afrikan selves. The devastation wrought by modern day Sambos does not stop at the borders of the United States or any of the island nations. Slave culture from the United Kingdom, the United States, and the Caribbean is also being shoved down their throats. Rap is extremely popular in Afrika. Millions of misguided Afrikan youth are now learning to delight in the desecration of their traditions and their humanity. Gangsta rappers are teaching Afrikan boys to treat women like garbage. The rank sexuality in mainstream rap lyrics and videos further fuels the spread of HIV. Black people everywhere are at a crossroads. We are pleased to report that Afrikan nations show evidence of a return to their natural cultures. Instead of degrading their women, Afrikans are looking to sisters for leadership and new direction. In 2005, Ellen Johnson-Sirleaf of Liberia became the first elected female president of an Afrikan country. We find several examples of what is possible when Black people reject the limitations of the slave mind in her career. She began her career as an Accountant. Our sister served as Minister of Finance for the Government of Liberia from 1980–1985. From 1982–1985, she also served as Vice President of the Afrika Regional Office of Citibank (Nairobi) and as Vice President of the Executive Board of Equator Bank in Washington, DC. She has received the Franklin Delano Roosevelt Freedom of Speech Award, the Ralph Bunche International Leadership Award, and the Grand Commander Star of Afrika Redemption. Also called the "Iron Lady", this Harvard-educated sister was sentenced to 10 years in prison for speaking out against the military regime. President Sirleaf-Johnson was elected by a 20% margin of the vote. Without making any predictions about the efficacy of her presidency, we congratulate her for what she represents. Afrikan women are not the footstools of the race. They are respected scientists and powerful politicians. We have not surrendered our identity to the racists who have worked for centuries to make visions of disorder, disease, and poverty instantly spring to mind whenever one mentions Afrika. In fact, the beginning of the century brought a great deal of promise to the Continent. All over Atlantic Afrika, an oil boom has given the economies a much needed boost. In 2004, Chad and Mauritania joined the ranks of the oil-producing nations, a move that is predicted to revitalize the financial infrastructures of both countries. Equatorial Guinea, Angola, and Gabon also capitalized on the surge in oil. This trend illustrates the desire of many Afrikans to become serious contenders in the global market. It also demonstrates the availability of natural resources in Afrika and gives us hope that our people will soon be better equipped to utilize these resources to fund much-needed projects in medicine, construction and education.

Building a New Afrikan Marketplace

Our people continue to challenge the notion that we are market builders who cannot capitalize on our own inventions. In 2005, Lachelle Bender-Williams of Cleveland established the Gimme A Hand School of Manicuring. It is Ohio's first and only beauty school for manicurists. Other schools offer manicuring classes as part of a larger beauty program. Gimme A Hand School of Manicuring focuses solely on nail care. This allows sisters to corner the market on new techniques and nail styles. Our women conceptualize the various designs that are wildly popular today. They ought to benefit from what they have created. In 1999, Amy Hilliard combined her Howard education with her love of baking to create the Comfort Cake Company. She offers "gourmet, Southern-style cakes" in chocolate, lemon, vanilla, and a variety of flavors. Our sister also sells sugarless cakes for those who are dieting or stricken with diabetes. Her major clientele include US Airlines and the Chicago Public School District. While Ms. Hilliard deserves much of the credit for her courageous and shrewd endeavors, we certainly recognize the Afrikan elements of her success. She maintains the Comfort Cake Company as a family-run business. The company catchphrase, "Pound cake so good it feels like a hug", is the brainchild of her then 14 year-old daughter. Her son acts as the "chief taste tester", and the recipe for her cakes was handed down from her grandfather. Black families are havens for fresh talent. How many more Amy Hilliards are waiting in the wings? It is no secret that Afrikan women have an incredible talent for cooking and baking. When we let go of the falsified Afrikan identity, we also let go of fear. We become confident in our abilities. We are no longer satisfied with simply dreaming. We understand that it is our duty manifest reality; to weave our dreams into something that we can see, smell, and touch. This is what Black women do. The post-Pride mentality confines our women to strip joints, government housing, and jail cells.

Successful business management requires some degree of education. Without it, we will be eaten alive in the shark-infested sea that is the business world. Contrary to the anti-educational stance of today's rap music, we still yearn to learn. In 2005, 80% of Afrikans in the United States were high school graduates. 18% held advanced degrees. This is up 5% from 1997's figures. But education is about more than classrooms, laboratories, professors, and exams. The ranks of the self-taught are swelling exponentially. The middle-aged brother whose nose is always in a book as he rides the bus each day is self-taught. The young sister who cannot stop ordering books and documentaries online is self-taught. Our community owes a lot to independent scholarship. Much of what is known about our heritage has been provided by these free-thinkers, who often share their knowledge with the rest of us. Many of our brothers and sisters in the penal system self-educate as well. They turn the bitterness of long sentences into an opportunity to heal themselves and prepare their minds for the day when they are released. The Internet has truly been a blessing in this regard. Every week, new websites and blogs appear on the Web, posted by Afrikans who have fulfilled their duty by teaching themselves who we are. These are often the best and only sources for historical information on Afrika. Traditionalist websites explore our contributions to the Indian and Chinese civilizations like no single book to date. Biographies of little-known Black authors (such as Ann Petry and Paule Marshall), are also readily available online, thanks in large part to independent Black scholars. We owe it to ourselves to take advantage of this information.

The next generation must be equipped to carry the torch when their time arrives. The past 10 years have also brought Afrikan home-schooling to a growing number (10%) of Afrikan families. We understand the Public School System's inability to address the needs of our young people. We are taking responsibility for teaching them ourselves. There are several online outlets for information on home schooling Black children. One such website is African-American Unschooling. This site serves as an information hub, providing information on where to incorporate Afrikan culture into the home-schooling environment. They offer free Afrikan-centered study materials. CreativeFolk.com offers "Afrikan American Studies Toolkit" for children grades 6–12. The site also has a comprehensive set of links to recommended organizations. Many of them feature interactive games that teach mathematics, science, history, and geography. Some of the sites also offer Afrikan recipes from both the Continent and the Diaspora to enhance the learning experience. Launched in 2003 by Jennifer and Michael James, the National African-American Homeschoolers Alliance (NAAHA) is a website that promotes quality Afrikan-centered books and curriculum. NAAHA is a nonsectarian organization with Muslim, Christian, and Buddhist membership. Their site is updated regularly and encourages participation from its users. With or without help from the system, we are determined to wrestle our Afrikan minds free from the suffocating stranglehold of ignorance. There are also several websites owned by organizations dedicated to enhancing the experience of Black motherhood. Mocha Moms Online is a support group for stay at home Black mothers. It is a sizeable organization directed by a National Executive Board. Georgia alone is home to 14 of its chapters. Mocha Moms operates in 15 states. The site provides information on breastfeeding, health and nutrition. There are also articles on how to manage finances, home schooling, and political advocacy.

Taking back our minds naturally leads to deeper respect for our bodies. We begin to consider health issues from an Afrikan perspective. We begin to understand that Afrikan people pay the heaviest toll for eating the very foods that are most heavily marketed in our neighborhoods. We are the ones most often stricken with diabetes, gout, hypertension, and sleep apnea. We are showing in increasing numbers that we want to be well off- not just financially, but physically as well. Afrikans in the West are turning to exercise and non-Western diets instead of letting the commercials dictate what we eat. Consequently, there has been a resurgence of Black-owned restaurants that provide nutritionally sound meals. One such establishment is Tchefa Nefer, a Pennsylvania-based eatery. Their menu is composed of animal-free cuisine made from high-quality vegetables, soy, and wheat. BeHealthyLifestyles.com is an organization which promotes health consciousness in the Black community. It debuted in 1999 at the Congressional Black Caucus Legislature Weekend. The website has information for people of all ages, include a game zone with activities that teach our children how to eat healthy and stay fit. The site also focuses on health concerns that are specific to the Afrikan community, such as asthma, diabetes, and hypertension. There is also BlackDoctor.org. This comprehensive website offers fantastic exercise tips, particularly for Black men. The routines are designed to enhance the Afrikan physique. BlackDoctor.org also features dietary information and mental health resources. Equally important is the national database of Black doctors on the site. By entering one's zip code, one is able to find a Black doctor or dentist in their area. It is especially important for our children to see Afrikan people working as physician, dentists, and scientists. In 2006, Queen Afua launched her "Nutrition Kitchen Malibu Retreat". The theme of this California gathering was the medical and spiritual benefits of healthy eating. Llaila O. Afrika treated us to valuable insights on the destructive nature of food in her courageous book entitled *Nutricide: The Nutritional Destruction of the Black Race*. These and countless other examples demonstrate our refusal to live the fractured existence meted out to us by the media. The 1960's were not the end of progressive cooperation among Black people. Technology may have altered the ways in which we communicate, but the will and the spirit remain the same.

Taking Care of Our Own

We rail against the Post-pride identity. Seeing ourselves as murderous niggas and insatiable whores does not inspire confidence in our race. This only prolongs our psychological enslavement. If Black people learn that we are incapable of helping ourselves and each other, we won't even try. This leaves the injustices of the status quo unchallenged. It is a strategy that existed long before rap music. But mainstream hip pop artists have chosen to perpetuate this myth by glorifying Black-on-Black violence. According to them, Black people should run away rather than towards one another. Today, many artists refuse to be two-dimensional cartoon characters. They are incredibly strong and compassionate people who are neither afraid nor ashamed to take care of our own. Rapper Warren G was not worried about appearing "soft" when he helped to establish the Willie McGinest Freedom School, a summer program that helps young people sharpen their literacy skills while raising cultural awareness. The project is part of a national program that is supported by the Children's Defense Fund. In 2005, Nashville rapper David "Young Buck" Brown generously supported Metro's Advancement Via Individual Determination Program. This is an initiative is directed at young people who would be the first in their families to ever attend a college or university. It focuses on their high school years, preparing them mentally and academically for success in the collegiate atmosphere. Midwest rapper Gapp Dwella (whose name is symbolic of bridging the gap between man and God) uses his experiences and religious training to minister to young people in the Ann Arbor, Michigan area. Jamaican artist Peter Lloyd once made appearances on sexploitation reggae-rap tracks. Now he does songs such as *Wake Dem Up*. He told Yardflex.com that he has "put away childish things" and is now ready to take his place among men. He hopes that his conscious songs will inspire Black youth to reject smoking, drinking, and curb their television habit. It is refreshing to know that there are a few brothers in the rap world whose interests in our children go beyond exploitation.

Our behavior in the aftermath of Hurricane Katrina tells a story of cooperation and endurance. Though the media reported mass confusion in the affected areas, Black men and women began to organize very quickly. Lieutenant General Russell Honore', a graduate of historically Black Southern University, was part of the first wave of effective efforts to maintain order in New Orleans. He immediately ordered police and soldiers to point their weapons at the ground; casting himself as a barrier between our people and a trigger-happy, overworked, and frustrated police force. Brigadier General Robert Crear (also recipient of the Black Engineer of the Year Award in 2003), managed to solve problems that the "experts" predicted would not be possible for several weeks. His plan involved blocking the gaps in two levees so that the water removal efforts (via pumping) could begin. Black people were not just stealing and begging for help. And while many stores were emptied of their goods, the items taken were overwhelmingly necessities such as food and clothing. Afrikans have a unique appreciation for justice and order. Having been denied both for several centuries has made us an empathetic and protective people. We do not descend into rioting and chaos at every opportunity. We are perfectly capable of policing ourselves.

Many Black celebrities rushed to the aid of our disaster-stricken people in the South as well. Jamie Foxx and Macy Gray were among the first people on the ground in the affected areas. They delivered food and supplies. Equally important was the message that their presence sent. We care about our own. Oprah Winfrey provided vital medical staff and equipment to the elderly and injured. Rappers Master P, Silkk the Shocker, and Lil' Romeo planned a benefit tour. Master P. also created a charity called Team Rescue that collected food, clothing, and cash funds for Katrina victims. Those of us who followed the news media coverage of the disaster were told a different story. We were called "refugees" in a country that our grandparents built. We were portrayed as violent thieves and killers. Cameras focused on the broken storefront windows of electronics and footwear stores, always careful to show a few Black people walking by in the background or standing nearby. Images of our people standing on the streets, chanting "We want help" flooded the airwaves for weeks. The coverage of good Samaritans was largely focused on Caucasians. We were not given information about the members of the African Methodist Church that took complete strangers into their homes at their own expense. We heard nothing about our sister Carmen Spooner, the Program Manager at the Office of Community Services in Louisiana. She worked tirelessly with the National Center for Missing and Exploited Children, personally connecting 7 children with their families who were in shelters hundreds of miles away. Spooner contacted Flight America and coordinated their transportation. As a result, three families were quickly reunited. Spooner was also an evacuee herself. She worked for hours on end to help our people even though she could not return to her own home and was still unsure of the welfare of her own family and friends. Little was said about the generosity of Afrikan people in Texas, some of whom were housing upwards of 25 evacuees at one time. Dwight Brashear's name was not mentioned on the cable news networks, but this CEO and General Manager of Capital Area Transit System organized the use of hundreds of buses to evacuate hurricane victims. He coordinated the removal of thousands during the critical days following the disaster. We confronted the hurricane with strength, courage, compassion, and vigilance. We refused to be living stereotypes.

Every news feature on Afrika shows unkempt, malnourished Black people who are waiting for Americans and Europeans to come and rescue them. But in 2004, the majority of the food aid in Afrikan countries *was paid for by national governments*. They responded to the food crises not by begging, but by utilizing what they had in the best way possible. Recent years have also brought promising new initiatives such as Nigeria's plan to triple its rice production by 2007 and land reforms in Namibia. Afrikan people are waking up, embracing consciousness, and working to improve our lives. In Liberia, business executive Amos Smith awarded 22 scholarships to civil servants in 2006. Recipients were given six months of computer software training at the Afrikan Union Global Net Institute. In his comments to the Monrovia *Analyst*, Mr. Smith explained that the private sector can be just as effective at stimulating economic growth and technological development as the government. He went on to describe his gesture as one of "goodwill to help the nation and its people recover from conflict by creating a crisis-free environment" in Liberia. Our brother concluded his remarks by appealing to the youth of the country to "denounce violence and destructive tendencies" and to "return to the classrooms". Amos Smith is setting a fine example for Black people everywhere. A single person with courage and patience can create opportunities that endure for generations.

Sadly, reggae music has fallen under the sway of the manufactured Afrikan identity. Our people on the islands also suffer from the effects of this destructive mentality. In 2005, MTV launched *Tempo*, a music channel that promotes self-hatred and encourages coonish behavior in Jamaica. But MTV cannot break the forward momentum that is building on the islands. In Jamaica, the Bluefields Peoples Community Association (BPCA) is using innovative and ecologically responsible methods to improve their economy. The group is made up of farmers, fishermen, local store owners and residents. They understand that the state of their economy rests with tourism. But tourism imposes a heavy toll on the islanders' lifestyle. Large-scale construction increases pollution in the air, water, and soil. It also devours all of the farm land. The BPCA solved this problem by using solar energy. They use the sun to heat their water and as an alternative to electricity. This minimizes the damage to the island and allows the villagers to build hotels that run on solar power instead of stringing up miles of electrical wires and putting their wildlife at risk. Jamaican people care about much more than smoking marijuana, drinking rum, and parading Black women around as if they were sex slaves. Our brothers and sisters are solving their problems intelligently and with independent thinking. Brothers and sisters in Afrika are also becoming vigilant about the state of the environment. Soil depletion is a serious problem in Afrika. Many areas are overfarmed. The land is not producing the minerals needed to replenish itself. 40% of Afrika's Gross National Produce comes from agriculture. They realize they stand to lose a great deal if the land is not protected. In 2004, Dr. Wangari Mathai became the first Afrikan woman to receive a Nobel Prize for her work in agriculture and ecology. Her Greenbelt Movement has been a vehicle for the education and empowerment of Afrikan women since the early 1970's. This organization prepares Black women for entrepreneurship by providing them with agricultural education. These women go on to open small and medium-sized businesses of their own, selling products such as fruit, jam, and seeds. They also sell bundles of firewood and lumber for construction. More than 30 million trees had been planted by the time she received her prestigious award. Afrikans in the United States also show a growing resistance to the post-Pride mentality. One of the most promising developments to arise from the 2005 Millions More Movement was the Covenant with Black America. The Covenant provides an outline for progress in the American Black community, but can be modified and utilized by any Afrikan group. The book, *Covenant with Black America* reached number one on the New York Times best seller list in April of 2006. The message of the book is personal responsibility. Ultimately, we are all responsible for ourselves. What we need most is a community made up of intelligent, active, responsible individuals.

Remembering Afrika

Over the past 30 years, Afrikan people have intensified our efforts to reclaim our lost heritage. Black people in every corner of the globe are tapping into the strength and beauty of our roots. Afrikan Youth In Norway (AYIN) was founded in 1998. This organization offers a comprehensive range of activities for Black children and teens. Programs include field trips, and cultural celebrations. They have workshops on how to care for Black hair and skin, and history lessons. R.I.S.E. (Revolutionary, Independent, Solid, and Eloquent) is just one of the many projects promoted by AYIN. This initiative introduces young people to the music industry and encourages them to develop as artists. In 2003, R.I.S.E. released *Maroon*, a CD featuring more than 30 young Black rappers and singers. Their single, "All About the Benjamins" was a smash hit on radio and video charts in Norway. In Gambia, the International Roots Foundation (IRF) continues to celebrate their Roots Cultural event twice annually. Their stated purposes are showcasing Gambian culture to people all over the world and reuniting people of Afrikans in the Diaspora with their Ancestral Afrikan Motherland. They promote Afrikan unity. The forward movement in the Black community knows no borders. It is growing, evolving, and expanding. Our awakening is a universal one.

Between 1622 and 1639, 23,500 Afrikans were brought into what is now Mexico by Spanish colonizers. The descendants of these captives make up a small percentage of the Mexican population. Many openly acknowledge and revere their Afrikan heritage. A group called Mexico Negro is now pushing to have a racial breakdown added to the 2010 Mexican Census. They want to stand up, be counted, and organize for the preservation of our culture. Our people in Sao Paolo, Brazil are also returning to their roots. Though Brazil boasts the largest Black population outside of Continental Afrika, their history has been ignored. Brazil considers itself a land of racial equality, and the prevailing opinion among non-Afrikans is that there is no need to discuss race or ancestry. But in 2005, Afro-Brazilian pop singer and businessman Jose de Paula Neto launched *TV da Gente* (Our TV). It is the first Brazilian television network ever to be owned and operated by Afrikans. The programming is Afrikan-oriented, with quotations from Afro-American Civil Rights figures such as Martin Luther King read regularly as "Thoughts Of the Day". De Paula Neto plans to offer programs featured on the Black Family Channel[49]. These shows are being translated and dubbed into Portuguese. Reclaiming our heritage eradicates the false barriers erected between Black people. It allows us to benefit from the wisdom of the total Afrikan experience. The Brazilian example highlights the love and respect that exists between Afrikans of all nationalities.

Even our little sisters in Panama are doing their part to free their Afrikan minds. The Muchachas Guias (Panama's version of Girl Scouts) now celebrate Black Panamanian Heritage Day with lectures and photo shows. PRODES (Centro de Estudio Para La Promocion del Desarrollo) provides the educational materials. The girls are shown photographs that depict Congo dancing. They learn about the types of labor performed by female captives. There is also a program on the evolution of Black fashion in Panama, with an extensive collection of dresses of the Afro-French style. In Puerto Rico, El Museo de Nuestra

---

49   Digital cable network owned by Evander Holyfield, Marion Jackson, and Cecil Fielder.

Raiz Africana (Museum Of Our African Roots) serves as an important bridge between Black Puerto Ricans and their Afrikan history. Black history was left out of Puerto Rican textbooks for centuries even though a significant percentage of Puerto Ricans are of Afrikan descent. El Museo de Nuestra Raiz Africana's presentations are especially thorough and well-researched. The exhibits help Black people explore their Yoruba and Bantu origins. They also provide vivid details of the treatment that Afrikan captives received at the hands of the Spanish. There is a vivid presentation about the Middle Passage. A series of paintings tell the story of this three to four-month period of transit between Afrika and the Americas. Other attractions detail the lives of Black Puerto Ricans after slavery ended. There are photos and artifacts belonging to various Black island pioneers such as Rafael Cordero, who opened the first school for Afrikan children in Old San Juan.

The return to our roots has taken a unique form for many Afrikans in the United States and the Caribbean. Thousands of displaced Afrikans in the West are embracing traditional Afrikan religions. Some of us learn of these religions through independent study. They "discover" Western and Central Afrikan religions while researching our roots. Sometimes these seekers visit the Continent. They form lasting relationships with Afrikans who are willing to teach and assist them through the initiation process. Black people also become exposed to traditional Afrikan religions through Afrikan tourists, immigrants, and visiting scholars. Though many aspects of their religions are never disclosed to outsiders, many Afrikans are happy to share basic information with their cousins here in the West. A small percentage of us are born into households where traditional religion is practiced. These are typically the children of converts or Afrikan immigrants.

Nigerian-based religions are the fastest growing sect of Afrikan practices in America. The Yoruba faction is the largest. For most modern adherents, this goes above and beyond the practice of Afrikan religion simply because we are Afrikans. The Yoruba constitute a very large ethnic group. A sizeable percentage of the Afrikan-American population is of Yoruba descent. Many Black people have been able to ascertain, through genetic testing (such as the Afrikan Ancestry Project at Howard University) or genealogical research, that they truly are Yoruba. For them, Ifa is a natural choice. The United States is home to about a dozen Ifa-centered organizations. One of them is the Ile Ise Ejogbe Ife Ifa Temple. The temple's stated mission is to establish an Ifa community of people with integrity. They believe that this can be accomplished through strengthening our families and building "iwe pele" (good character). The temple is located in Maryland. It was established in 1999.

A significant percentage of Afrikans in the West can trace their origins to Ghana. The Adade Kofi Bosomfie Sankofa in Pennsylvania promotes Akan, one of the religions of Ghana. Adade Kofi Bosomfie Sankofa provides for all of its members' spiritual needs. Lessons in traditional Akan spirituals and dances allow the convert to practice in his or her home as well as in the temple. The center places a heavy emphasis on rites of passage ceremonies. Our community is in desperate need of a complete revival of this tradition. Popular culture has distorted what it means to be a human being. Black boys and girls find themselves unprepared for life as men and women. The lessons learned in rites of passage ceremonies help our young people develop a moral compass. This "compass" or set of standards acts as a measuring device for judging the correctness of behavior and ideas in the future. The Afrikan Women's Society holds regular WomenSpirit Celebrations as well. Another promising feature of Adade Kofi is the spiritual and psychological counseling. The Ausar-Auset Society was established in 1973. It promotes spiritual development through the religious methodologies of Ancient Kemet, Canaan, and Kush. This organization consists of an elaborate system of priests, priestesses, and kingships. Each branch of the Society operates autonomously. They offer courses in philosophy, meditation, nutrition, yoga, and astrology. There are centers in several states- Ohio, Pennsylvania, and DC for example. Black people are also showing a renewed interest in Diaspora-based religions, such as Shango and Cuban Orisha.

The Northern Star

The time to escape modern slavery has arrived. Afrikan people have suffered for far too long within the narrow constraints of this Willie Lynch-influenced, manufactured identity. We have at our disposal the only tool that will liberate us- Afrikan Soul. This Soul carries the imprint of 3.5 million years of intelligence, invention, and prosperity. The blessing of having been the first men and women to praise the Lord on this Earth is immense. We are the progeny of that small band of Black people that first learned to build shelters and to hunt. They passed on to us the most equitable and effective family system ever to have existed. They taught us that a community is a family. To this day, strangers in Afrika refer to one another as "cousin", "sister", or "uncle". Our ancestors were the first to use language. They were the first to sing and dance. They dammed rivers, crossed deserts beneath a merciless sun, and domesticated livestock. Ancient Afrikans left a treasure trove of wise folklore. Every problem that we face today is explained away in one of the many parables of West Afrika. We have only to embrace Afrika and She will continue to sustain. Afrika's most valuable treasures are invisible to the eye. It does not matter how much gold was stolen from Her soils by greedy Caucasians. It does not matter how deep the foolish Congolese government allows desperate China to mine its mountains. Only those that approach Afrika with love and respect in their hearts will know the true measure of Afrika's riches. Today, we are excellently equipped to discover, claim, and experience these luxuries.

The slave mind is captive to a brief period in our fantastic history. Today's Sambos suffer from stunted mental growth. They have no imagination except when it comes to inventing new ways to abuse Black women or destroying the Afrikan family. The post-Pride mentality can only offer us more addiction, disease, fatherless Black babies, and violence. Afrikan culture has given us Jazz, Ebonics, and the 360 Slam Dunk. It gave us the electric slide, the blood bank, and laser eye surgery. The tragic effects of slave culture dissolve and vanish in the ocean of natural Afrikan values. Our natural culture can return Black men to the home. It can stop the violence in New Orleans and Memphis. It can eradicate the petty differences between Afrikan Americans and Jamaicans, Igbo and Yoruba, Hutu and Tutsi. All we need to do is wash ourselves clean of the divisive and primitive ideas about how to achieve our individual goals. These notions of violence and injustice were foisted upon us by marauding foreigners. They do not belong to us. We must wash ourselves clean. Our eloquent ancestors said:

> *Jordan's water is chilly and cold*
> *God's gonna trouble the water*
> *It chills the body, but not the soul*
> *God's gonna trouble the water*

Wade in the water, children of Afrika! Each of us is the beloved child of Rupe, Allah, Tongnaab, Shango, Amma, Egun, Olokun, Christ, Chonganda, and Bisila. Has our Lord created niggas? Were we made to think and dwell in the meanest, most hopeless level of existence? Afrikan culture is a balm for what ails us. It is the prime elixir. The substance of our ancient culture is the ether from which sprang the first human soul. It is the Paradise of Adam and Eve, the flesh of the Nummo. It is the malanga fruit in Bisila's Hand. Knowing this makes it possible to wash ourselves clean. We may take off our masks and finally be free.

Wade in the water. Your name is not Nigga. You are the great grandson of the Magnificent Shamba Bolongogo, King of the Bakuba. This benevolent leader abolished all crude forms of warfare, including the throwing of daggers at the enemy. He brought weaving techniques to all of the Congo, including the introduction of the coveted raffia cloth. He ordered no home invasions, sold no crack, and did not permit prostitution in his country. Your great grandfather controlled an army that was 400,000 strong. Yet he said, "Kill neither woman, man, nor child. Are they not children of Chembe (God)?"

Your name is not Motherfucker. You are Sergeant Thomas Mc Phatter of the 8th US Marine Corps Ammunition Company, an all-Black regiment. You fought in World War II on the island of Iwo Jima. The Japanese surrounded your camp in 1945. They screamed "Bonsai!" and instantly began slicing through your canvas tents with their swords, severing arms and legs and draining the life blood from sleeping soldiers. Not once did you yell, "Yeah! Get them niggas!" You refused to tuck your tail and run away. You fought- unafraid and face to face- with soldiers whose training and experience far outweighed your own. When the smoke from your rifles cleared, you had eliminated them all. This was the last battle on Iwo Jima. Afrikan people did not start the tension between the Allies and Japan, but we certainly finished it.

Your name is not Bitch. Your name is Jackie Joyner Kersee. You were born in East St. Louis and the record you set at the 1988 Summer Olympics stands firm to this day. You conquered the hurdles, the shot put, the long jump and the javelin throw. You stood in a stadium in front of many thousands of people, with several million more watching at home. You looked the world in the eye and declared, "Yes, I can!" Wade in the water. Your name is not Hoe. You are Dr. Mae Jemison. You forged your career with hard work and determination. You became a doctor and returned to West Afrika, offering medical assistance to the poor. You learned to speak Swahili fluently and became a professional dancer. And you crowned your shining career with a trip beyond the stratosphere aboard NASA's 1992 Spacelab expedition. For 8 glorious days, you floated weightless above the Earth as you conducted research on bone cells. You were able to see that this world is absolutely beautiful when considered from the proper perspective. It is a place of infinite bounty, helping hands, love, and compassion.

If you get there before I do
God's gonna trouble the water
Tell my friends I'm coming too
God's gonna trouble the water